FINGERPICKING ACOUSTIC

INTRODUCTION TO FINGERSTYLE GUITAR 2

BEHIND BLUE EYES 6
BEST OF MY LOVE 12
BLOWIN' IN THE WIND 3
THE BOXER 16
DUST IN THE WIND 26
HELPLESSLY HOPING 30
HEY JUDE 34
IN MY LIFE 23
LEARNING TO FLY 38
LEAVING ON A JET PLANE 43
PATIENCE 46
TEARS IN HEAVEN 50
THIS LAND IS YOUR LAND 54
TIME IN A BOTTLE 57
YOU'VE GOT A FRIEND 60

T0055449

ISBN 978-0-634-06537-8

For all works contained herein:
Unauthorized copying, arranging, adapting, recording or public performance is an infringement of copyright. Infringers are liable under the law.

Visit Hal Leonard Online at www.halleonard.com

HAL•LEONARD® CORPORATION
7777 W. BLUEMOUND RD. P.O. BOX 13819 MILWAUKEE, WI 53213

INTRODUCTION TO FINGERSTYLE GUITAR

Fingerstyle (a.k.a. fingerpicking) is a guitar technique that means you literally pick the strings with your right-hand fingers and thumb. This contrasts with the conventional technique of strumming and playing single notes with a pick (a.k.a. flatpicking). For fingerpicking, you can use any type of guitar: acoustic steel-string, nylon-string classical, or electric.

THE RIGHT HAND

The most common right-hand position is shown here.

Use a high wrist; arch your palm as if you were holding a ping-pong ball. Keep the thumb outside and away from the fingers, and let the fingers do the work rather than lifting your whole hand.

The thumb generally plucks the bottom strings with downstrokes on the left side of the thumb and thumbnail. The other fingers pluck the higher strings using upstokes with the fleshy tip of the fingers and fingernails. The thumb and fingers should pluck one string per stroke and not brush over several strings.

Another picking option you may choose to use is called hybrid picking (a.k.a. plectrum-style fingerpicking). Here, the pick is usually held between the thumb and first finger, and the three remaining fingers are assigned to pluck the higher strings.

THE LEFT HAND

The left-hand fingers are numbered 1 though 4.

Be sure to keep your fingers arched, with each joint bent; if they flatten out across the strings, they will deaden the sound when you fingerpick. As a general rule, let the strings ring as long as possible when playing fingerstyle.

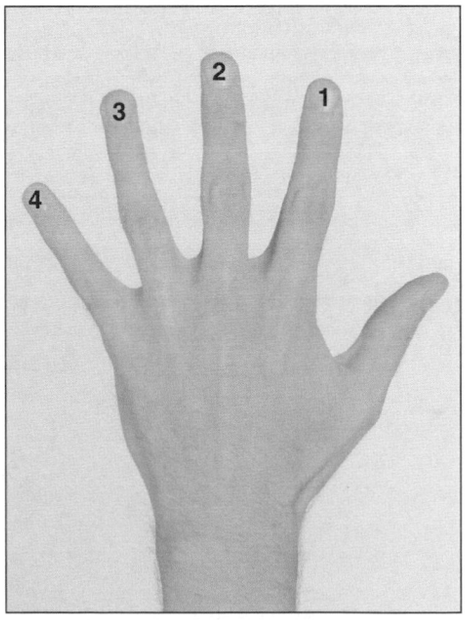

Blowin' in the Wind

Words and Music by Bob Dylan

Copyright © 1962 Warner Bros. Inc.
Copyright Renewed 1990 Special Rider Music
International Copyright Secured All Rights Reserved
Reprinted by Permission of Music Sales Corporation

G G/F# Em G C D
white dove sail be - fore she sleeps in the sand?

G C G
How man - y times must the can - non balls fly be -

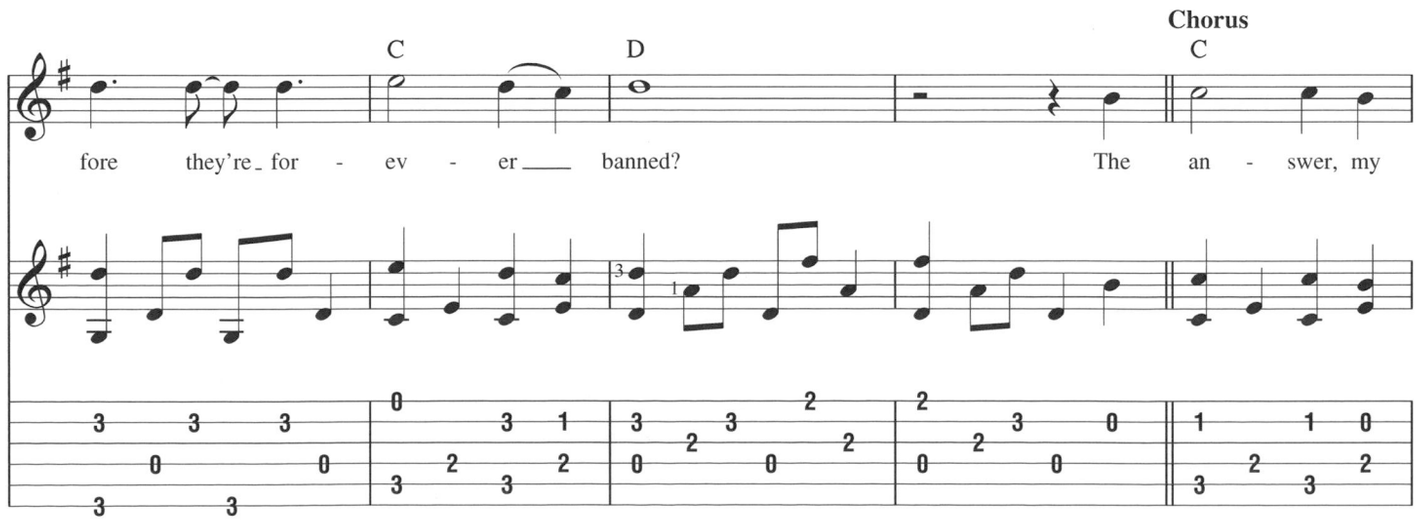
C D Chorus C
fore they're for - ev - er banned? The an - swer, my

Outro

Play 3 times

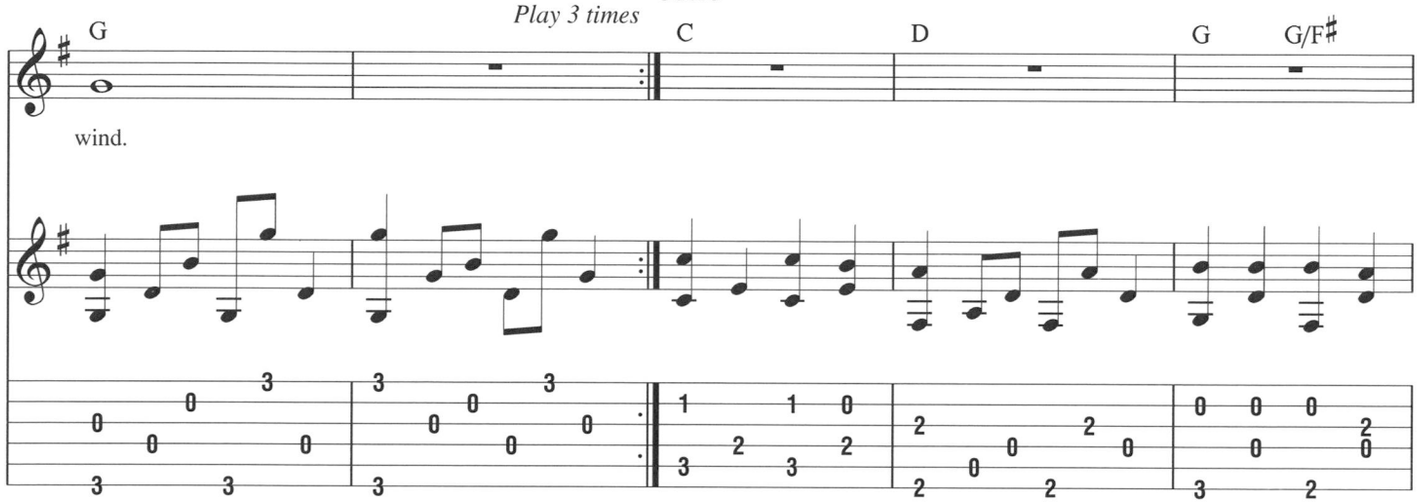

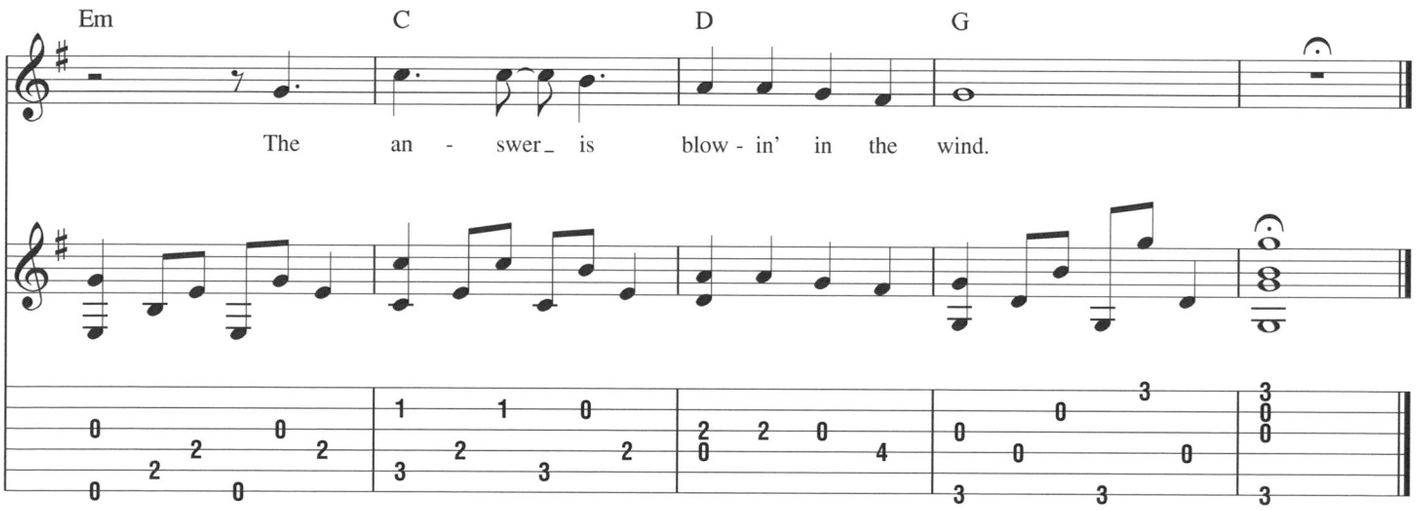

Additional Lyrics

2. How many years can a mountain exist
Before it's washed to the sea?
How many years can some people exist
Before they're allowed to be free?
How many times can a man turn his head,
And pretend that he just doesn't see?

3. How many times must a man look up
Before he can see the sky?
How many ears must one man have
Before he can hear people cry?
How many deaths will it take till he knows
That too many people have died?

Behind Blue Eyes

Words and Music by Pete Townshend

Copyright © 1971 by Towser Tunes, Inc., ABKCO Music and Fabulous Music Ltd.
Copyright Renewed
All Rights for Towser Tunes, Inc. Administered by BMG Music Publishing International
All Rights for BMG Music Publishing International in the U.S. Administered by Careers-BMG Music Publishing, Inc.
International Copyright Secured All Rights Reserved

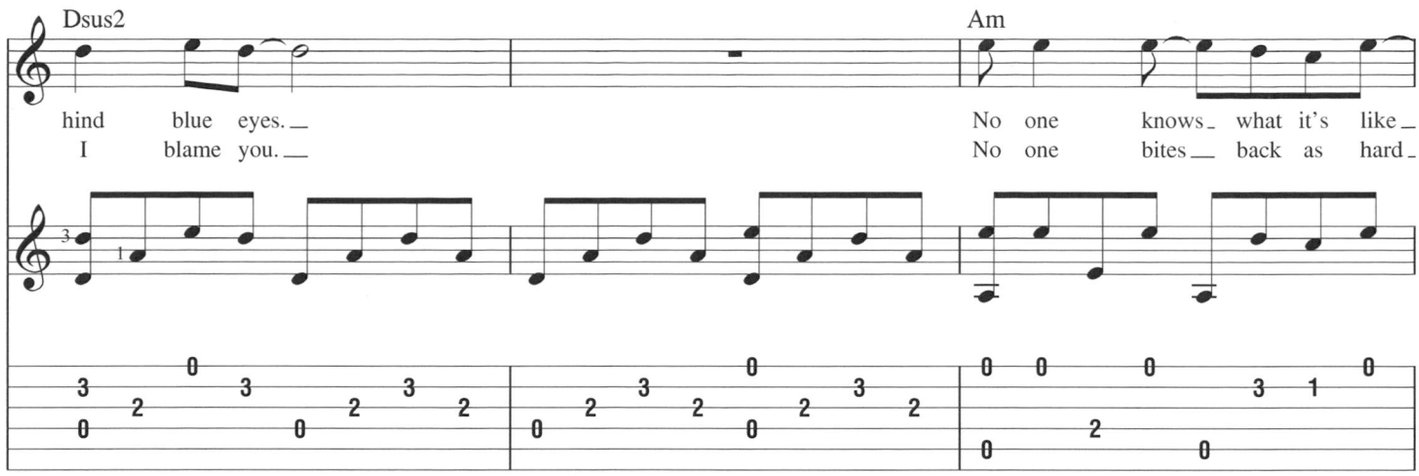
Dsus2
Am
hind blue eyes.
I blame you.
No one knows what it's like
No one bites back as hard

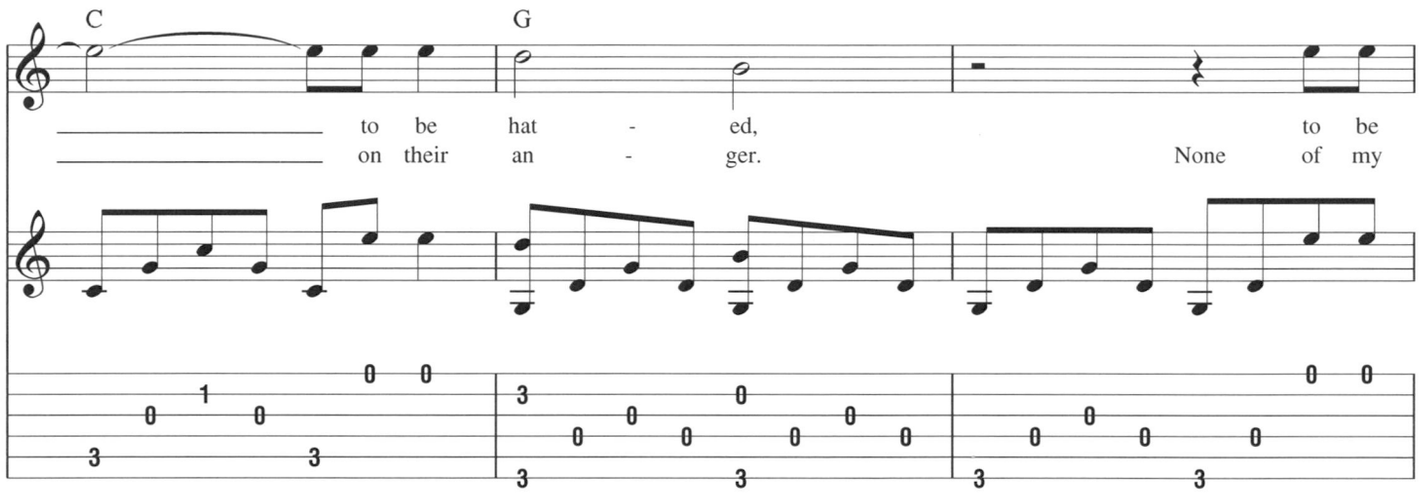
C
G
to be hat - ed, to be
on their an - ger. None of my

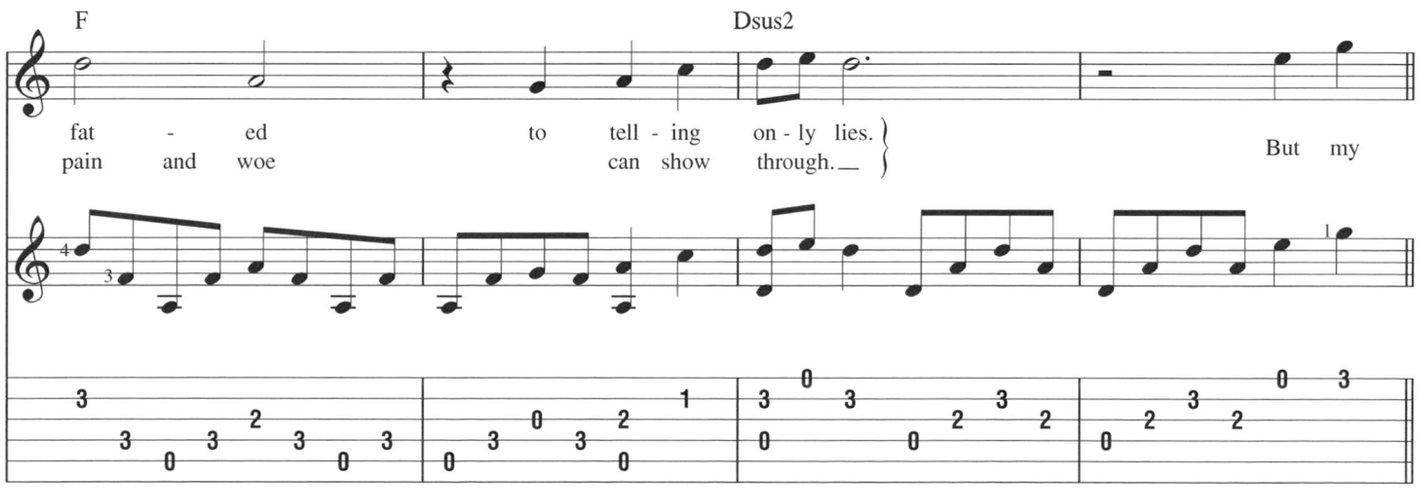
F
Dsus2
fat - ed to tell - ing on - ly lies.
pain and woe can show through.
But my

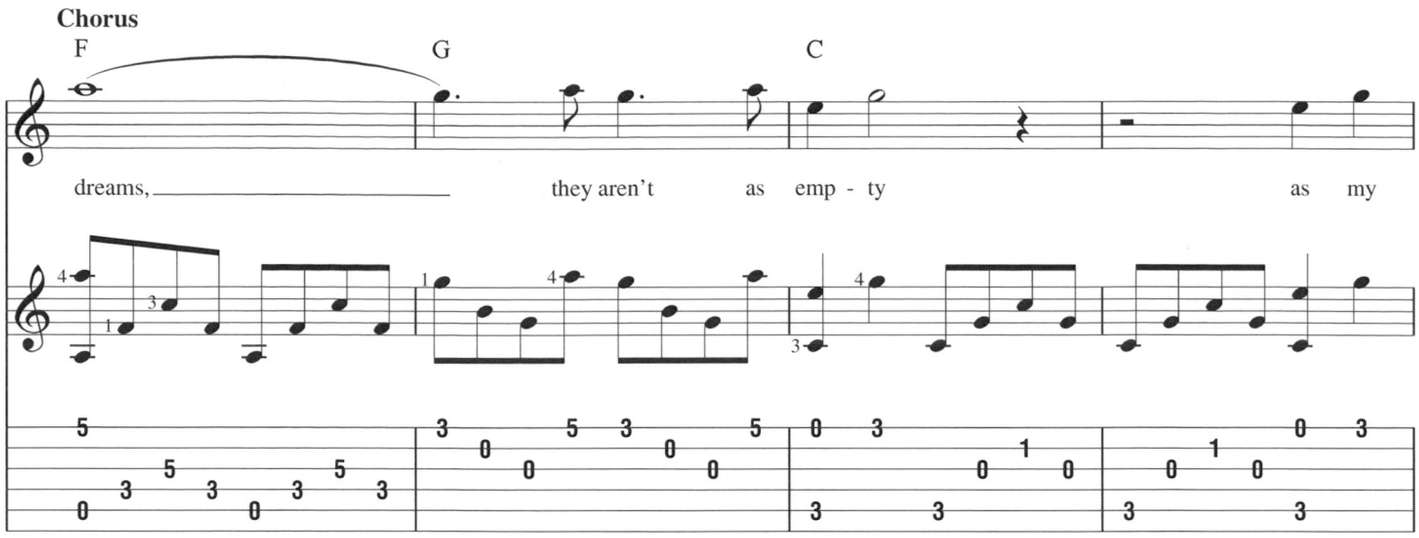
Chorus
F
G
C
dreams, they aren't as emp - ty as my

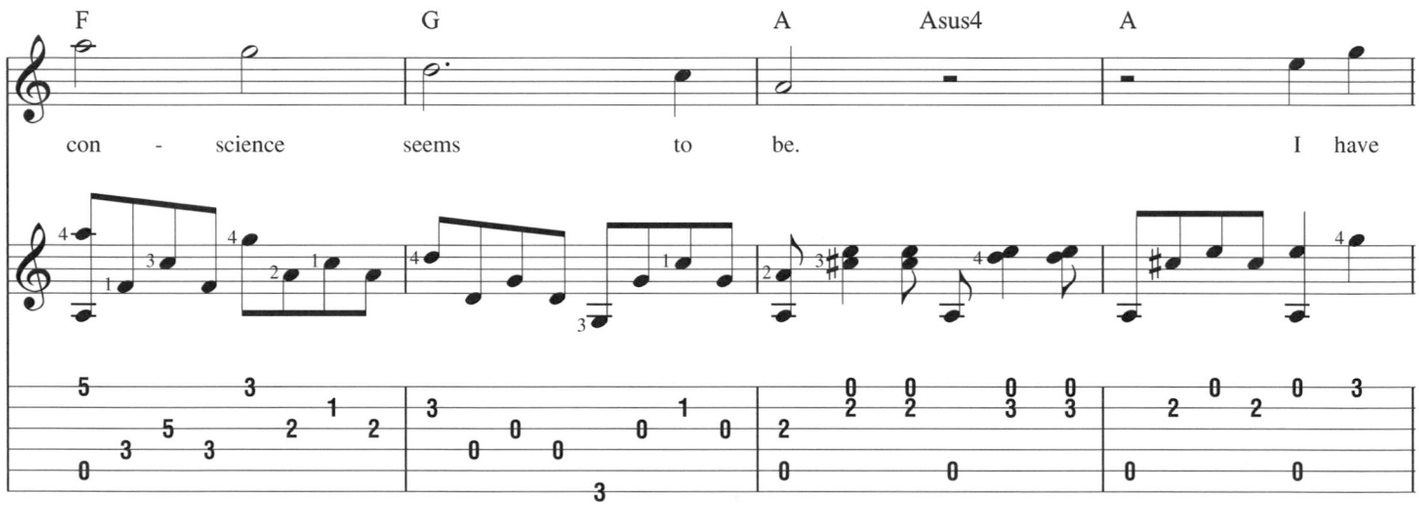
F
G
A
Asus4
A
con - science seems to be. I have

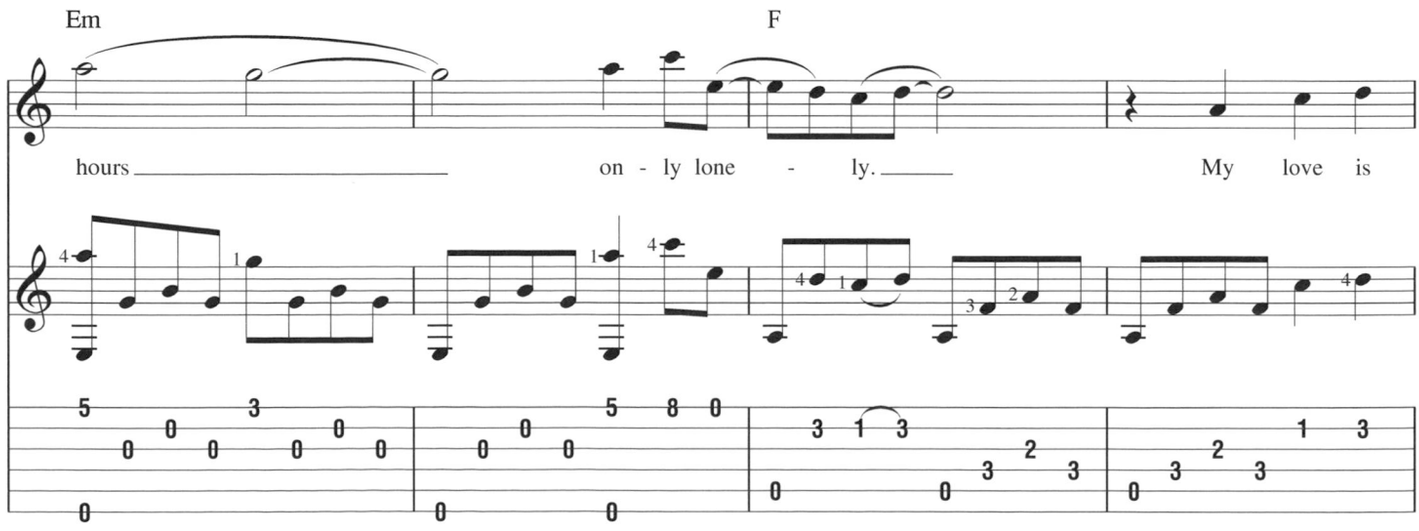
Em
F
hours on - ly lone - ly. My love is

G
Dsus2
ven - gence
that's nev - er free.
1.
2.
A
Em
D
A
Em
D
Verse
A
Em
D
A
3. When my fist clench - es,
crack it o - pen
be - fore I use

Em C G Em D
it and lose my cool. When I smile, tell me some bad
G Em D A Em D
news be-fore I laugh and act like a fool.
A Em D A
If I swal - low an - y thing e - vil, put your fin -
Em C G Em D
- ger down my throat. And if I shiv - er, please give me a

G
Em
D
A
blank - et. Keep me warm; let me wear your coat.
E
E/D
Outro
Am
No one knows what it's like
C
G
to be the bad man, to be the
F
Dsus2
sad man be - hind blue eyes.

Best of My Love

Words and Music by John David Souther, Don Henley and Glenn Frey

© 1974 (Renewed 2002) EMI BLACKWOOD MUSIC INC., CASS COUNTY MUSIC and RED CLOUD MUSIC
All Rights Reserved International Copyright Secured Used by Permission

Fmaj7
things that we said and com - in' a - part at the seams.
Em7
Dm7
Em7
We tried to talk it o - ver but the words come out too
F
C
Fmaj7
rough. I know you were try - in' to give me the best of your
To Coda
1.
2.
Chorus
C
G
G
C
love.
Whoa,
sweet

Dm7
dar - lin'.
You get the best of my
love.
Whoa,
1/3CI
C
Dm7
sweet dar - lin'.
You get the best of my
Bridge
Fm
love.
Oo,
I'm go - in' back in time
and it's a
1/3CI
1/2CI
1/2CI
Cmaj7
Fm
sweet dream.
It was a qui - et night,
and I would
1/2CI

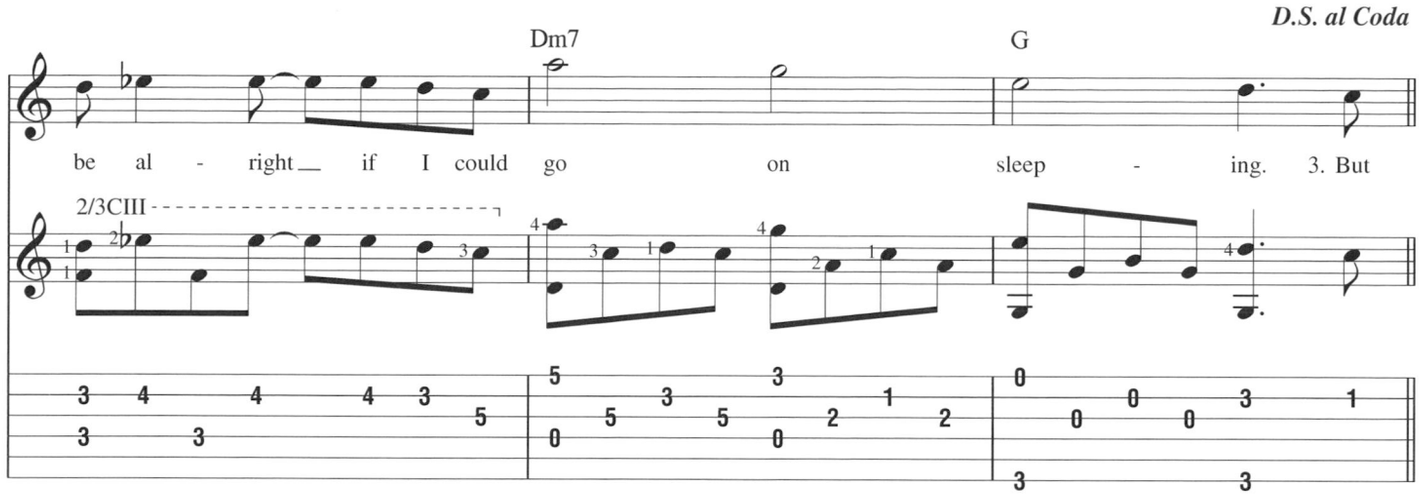

Additional Lyrics

2. Beautiful faces and loud empty places, look at the way we live.
   Wastin' our time on cheap talk and wine, left us so little to give.
   That same old crowd was like a cold, dark cloud that we could never rise above.
   But here in my heart, I give you the best of my love.

3. But ev'ry morning I wake up and worry what's gonna happen today.
   You see it your way and I see it mine but we both see it slippin' away.
   You know we always had each other, baby. I guess it wasn't enough.
   Oh, oh, but here in my heart, I give you the best of my love.

The Boxer

Words and Music by Paul Simon

Copyright © 1968 (Renewed) Paul Simon Music (BMI)
International Copyright Secured All Rights Reserved
Reprinted by Permission of Music Sales Corporation

1.
G
D/F♯
G
dis - re - gards the rest.
ged peo - ple go,
2. When I
2.
G
D/F♯
C
G
look - in' for the plac - es on - ly they would know.
Chorus
Em
D
Lie, la, lie.
Lie, la, lie, la, lie, la,

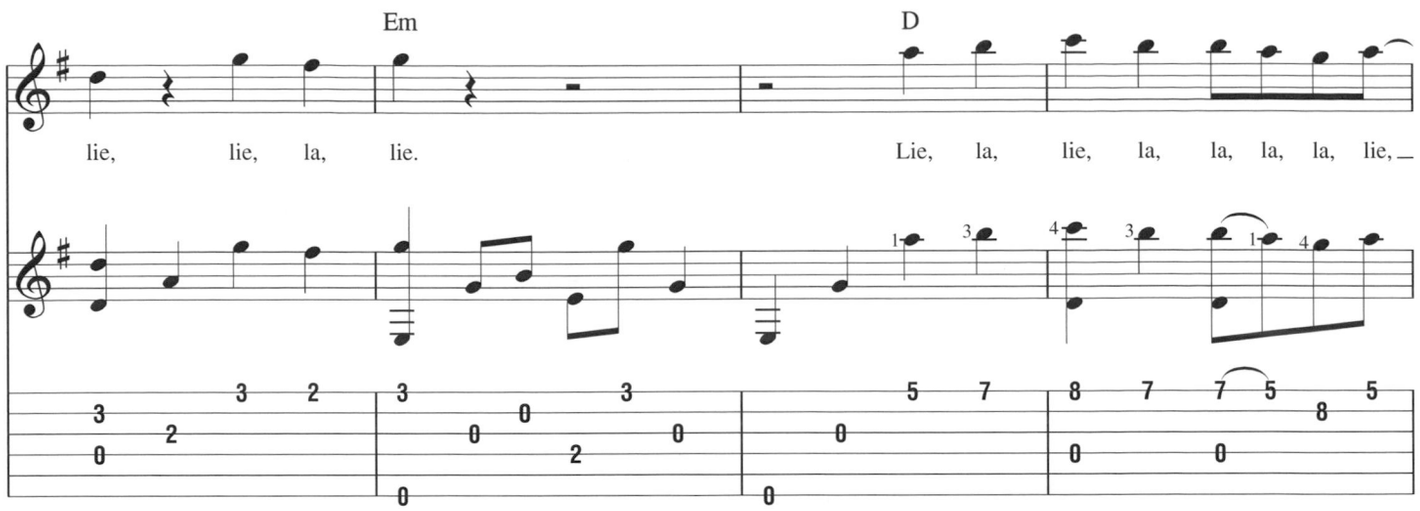
Em
D
lie, lie, la, lie.
Lie, la, lie, la, la, la, la, lie,

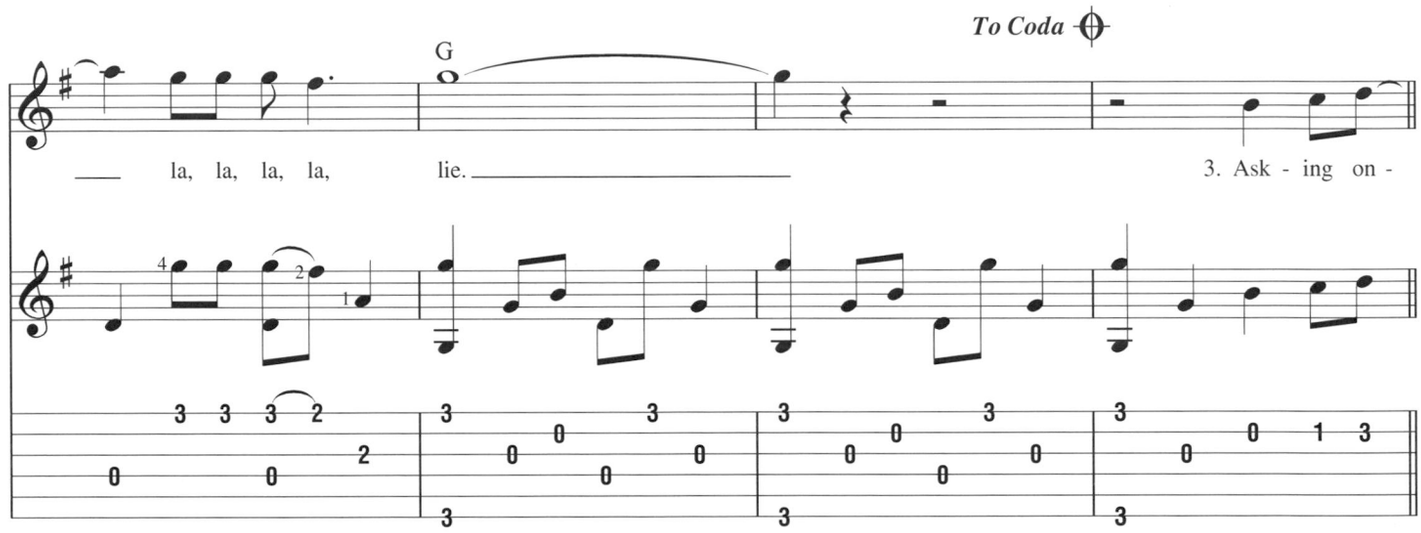
To Coda
G
la, la, la, la, lie.
3. Ask - ing on -

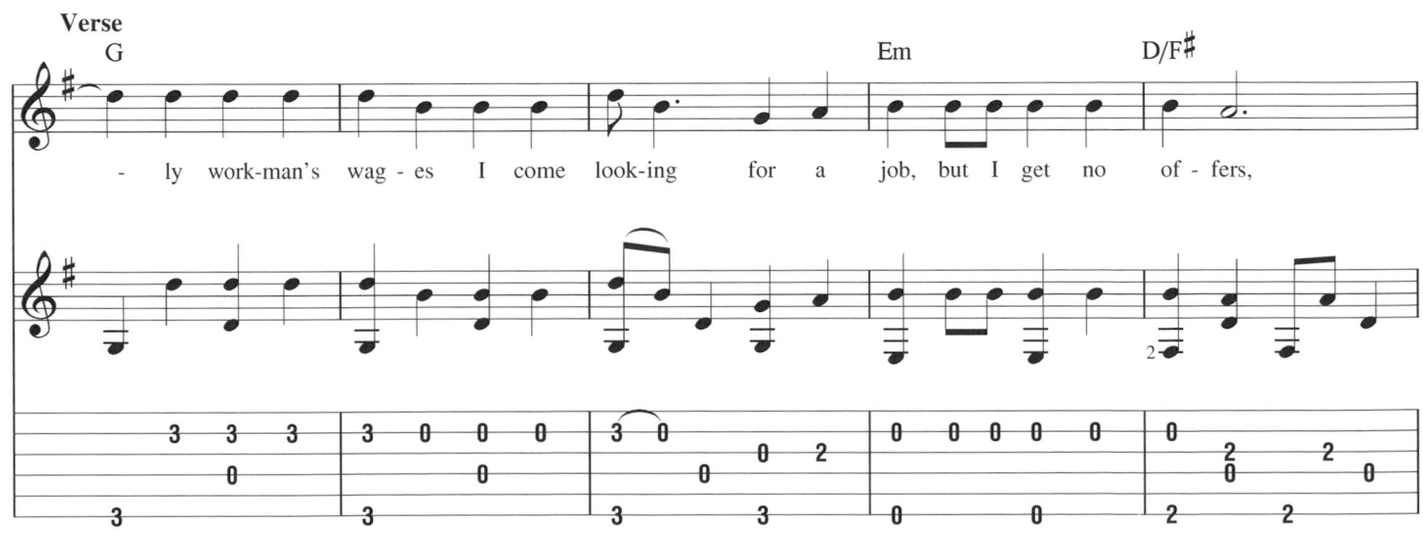
Verse
G
Em
D/F♯
- ly work-man's wag - es I come look-ing for a job, but I get no of - fers,

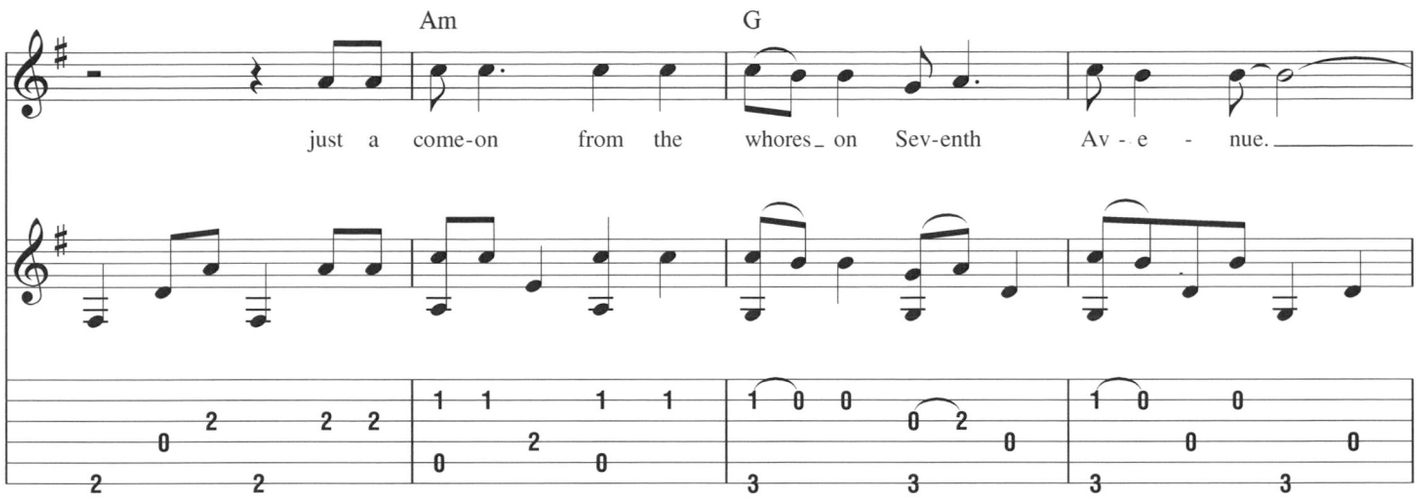
Am
G
just a come-on from the whores on Sev-enth Av - e - nue.

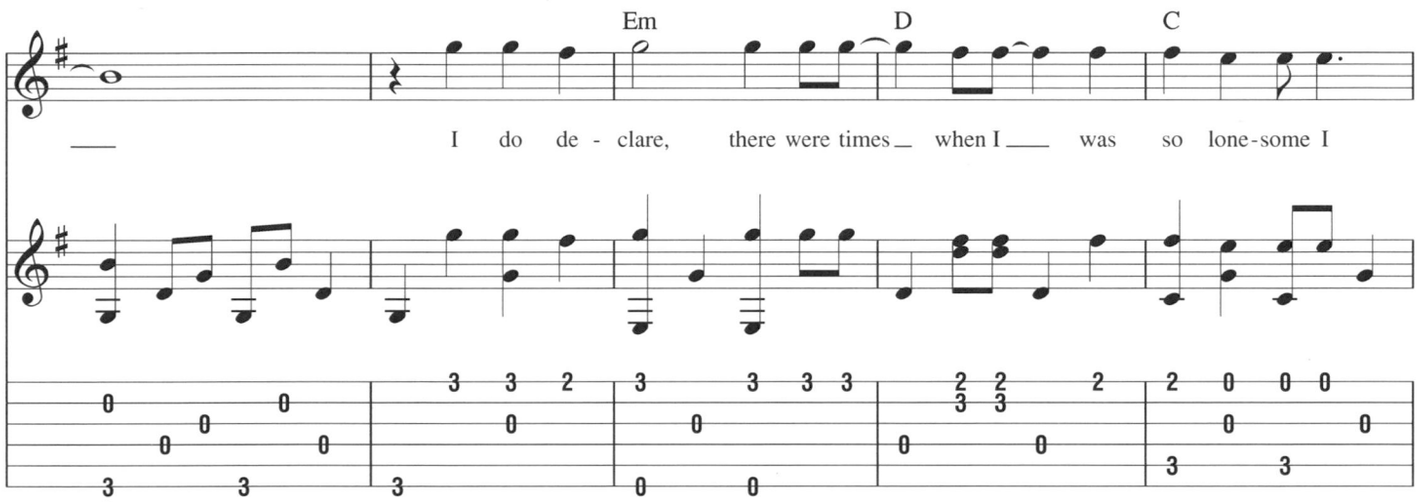
Em
D
C
I do de - clare, there were times when I was so lone-some I

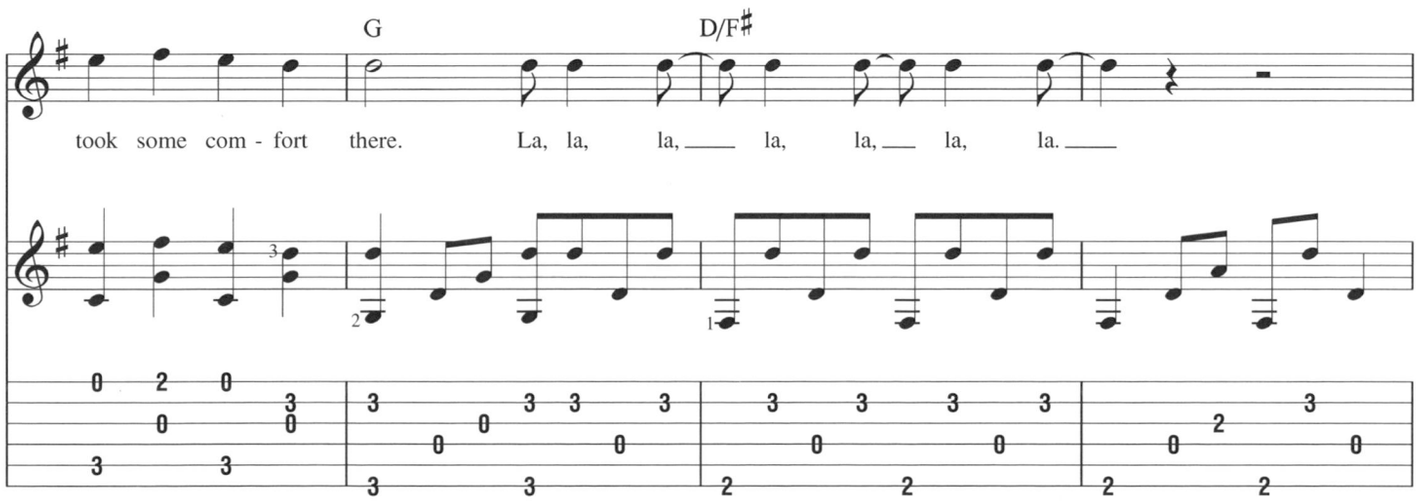
G
D/F♯
took some com - fort there. La, la, la, la, la, la, la, la.

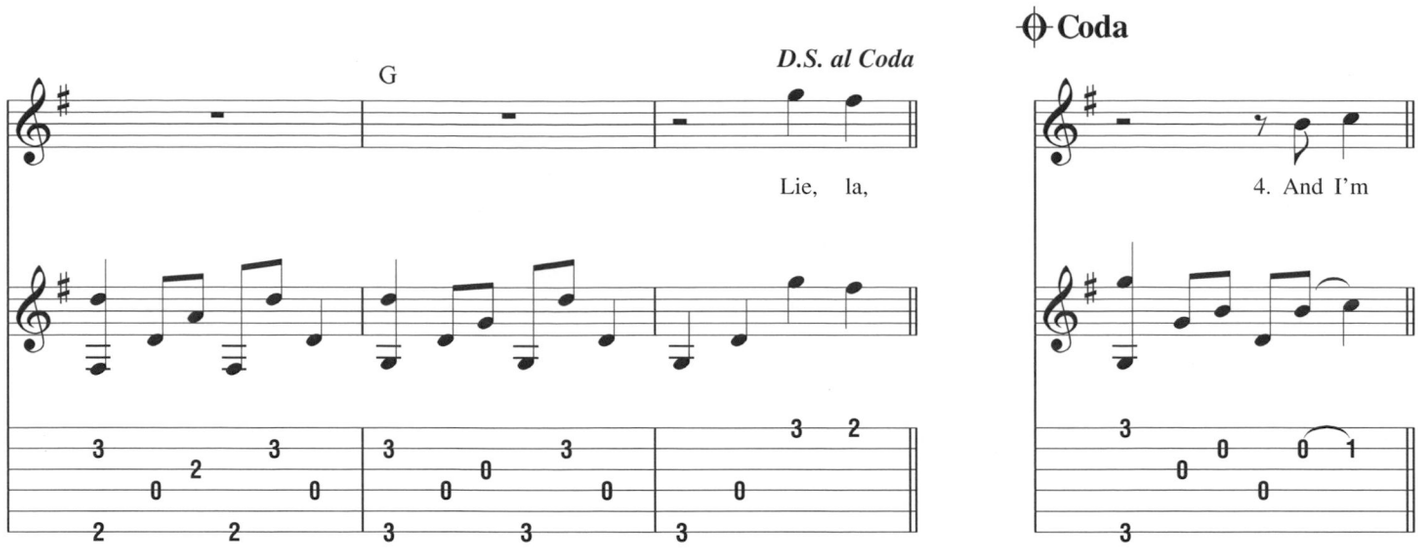
G
D.S. al Coda
Lie, la,
Coda
4. And I'm

Verse
G
Em
D/F♯
lay - ing out my win - ter clothes and wish - ing I was gone, go - ing home,

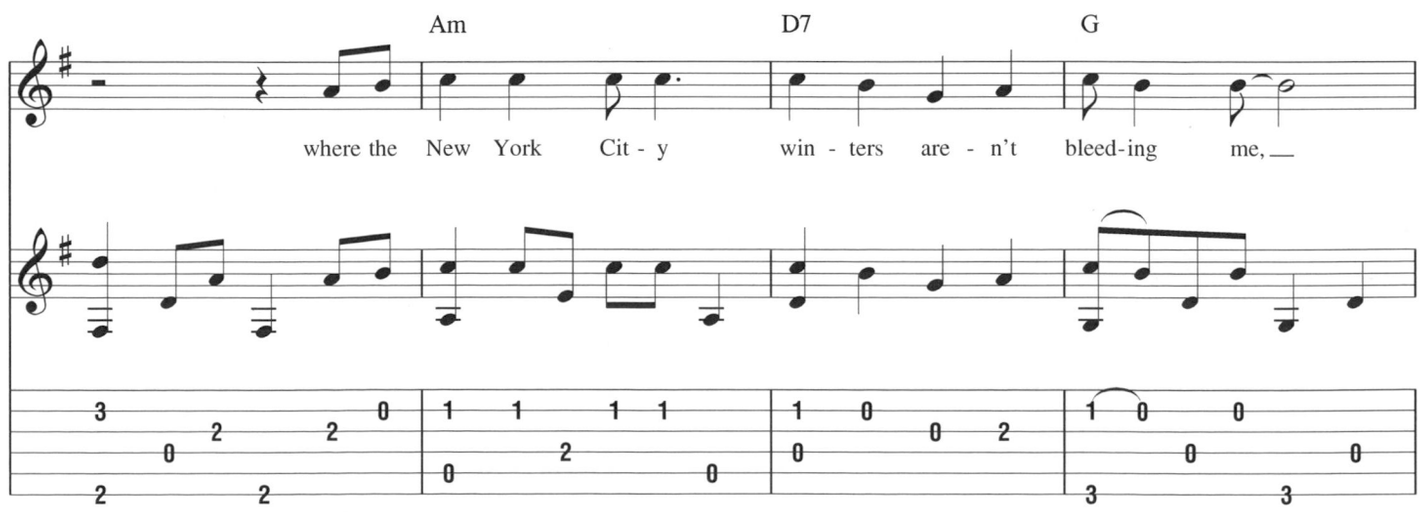
Am
D7
G
where the New York Cit - y win - ters are - n't bleed-ing me,

Bm7
Em
lead - ing me,
D/F♯
G
go - ing home.
5. In the
Verse
G
Em
D/F♯
clear - ing stands a box - er, and a fight - er by his trade, and he car - ries the re-mind-
D7/F♯
G
- ers of ev - 'ry glove that laid him down or cut him till he cried out in his

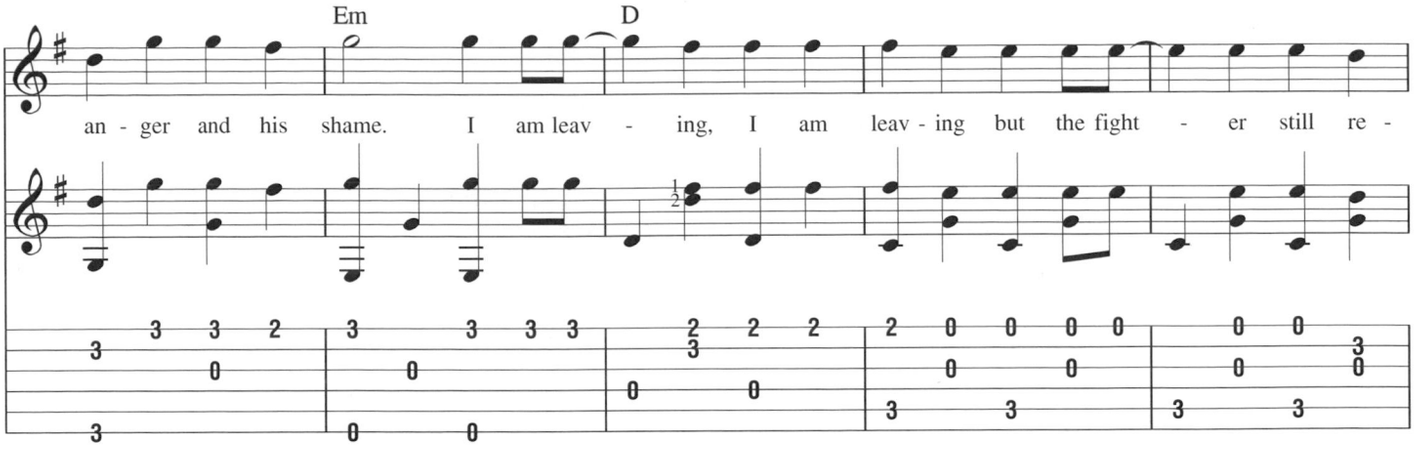
Em
D
an - ger and his shame. I am leav - ing, I am leav - ing but the fight - er still re -

Outro-Chorus
G
Em
D
mains. Lie, la, lie. Lie, la, lie, la, lie, la,

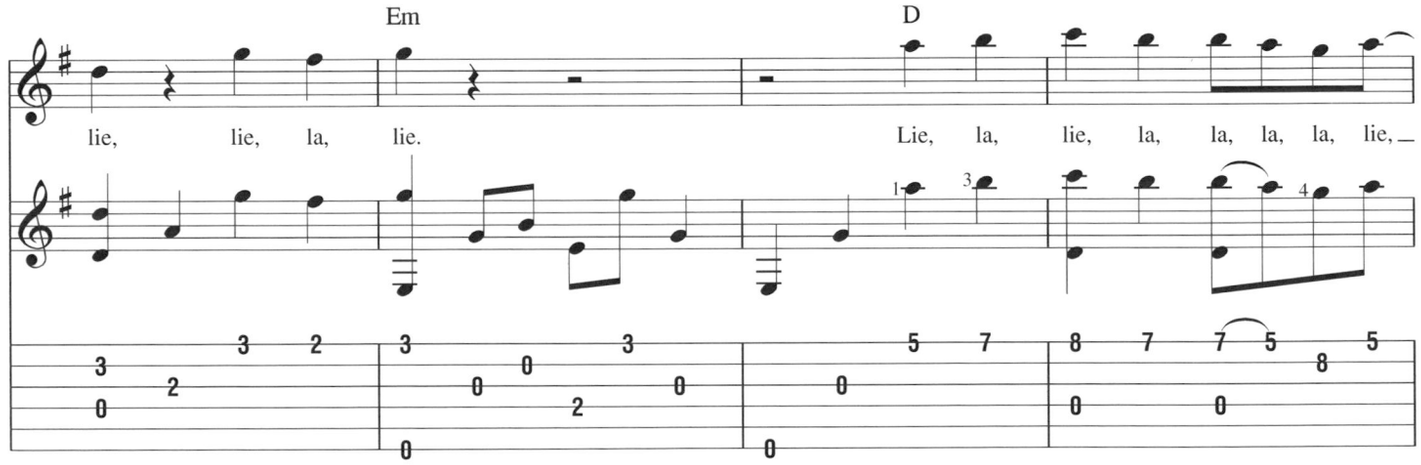
Em
D
lie, lie, la, lie. Lie, la, lie, la, la, la, la, lie,

G
1.
2.
la, la, la, la, lie. Lie, la,

In My Life

Words and Music by John Lennon and Paul McCartney

Copyright © 1965 Sony/ATV Songs LLC
Copyright Renewed
All Rights Administered by Sony/ATV Music Publishing, 8 Music Square West, Nashville, TN 37203
International Copyright Secured All Rights Reserved

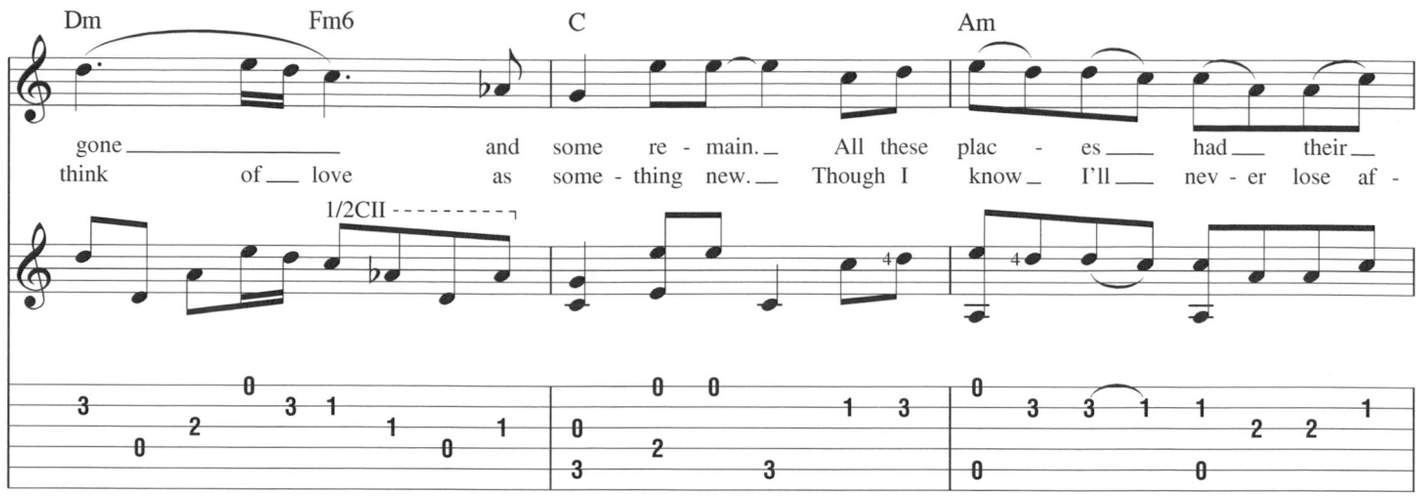
Dm
Fm6
C
Am
gone and some re - main. All these plac - es had their
think of love as some - thing new. Though I know I'll nev - er lose af -
1/2CII

F
B♭
C
mo - ments with lov - ers and friends I still can re - call. Some are
fec - tion for peo - ple and things that went be - fore. I

Am
D7
Fm6/A♭
dead and some are liv - ing. In my life I've
know I'll of - ten stop and think a - bout them. In my life I

1.
C
G
2.
C
loved them all.
2. But of love you more.

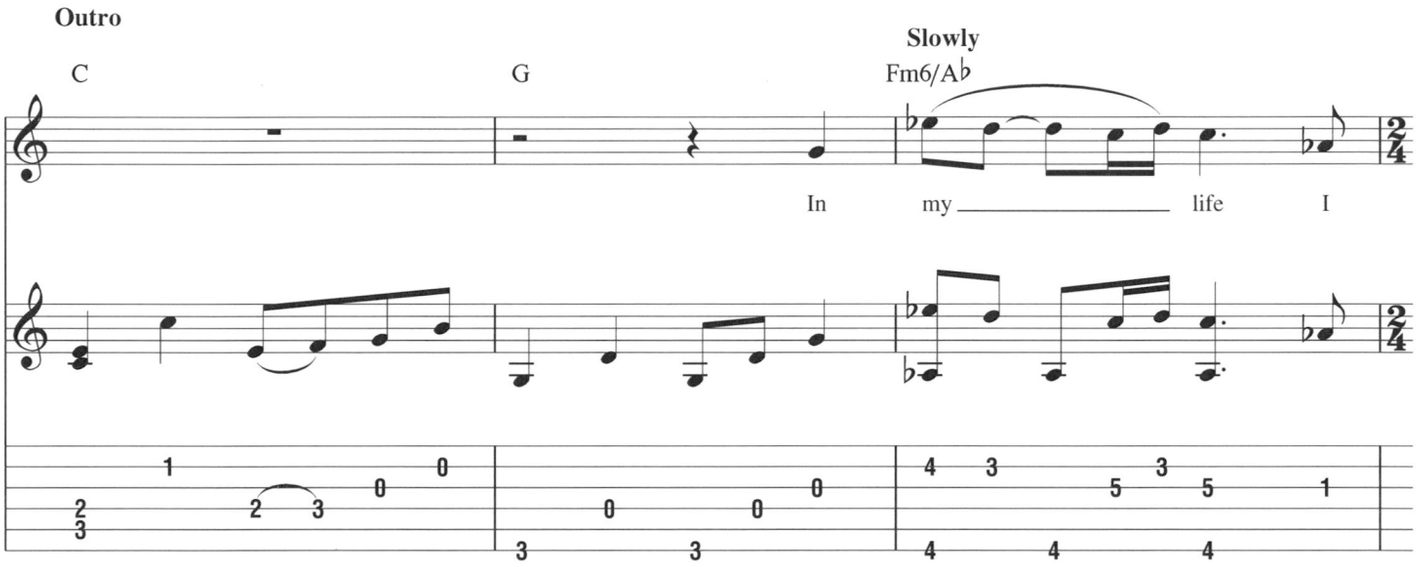
Outro
C
G
Slowly
Fm6/A♭
In my life I

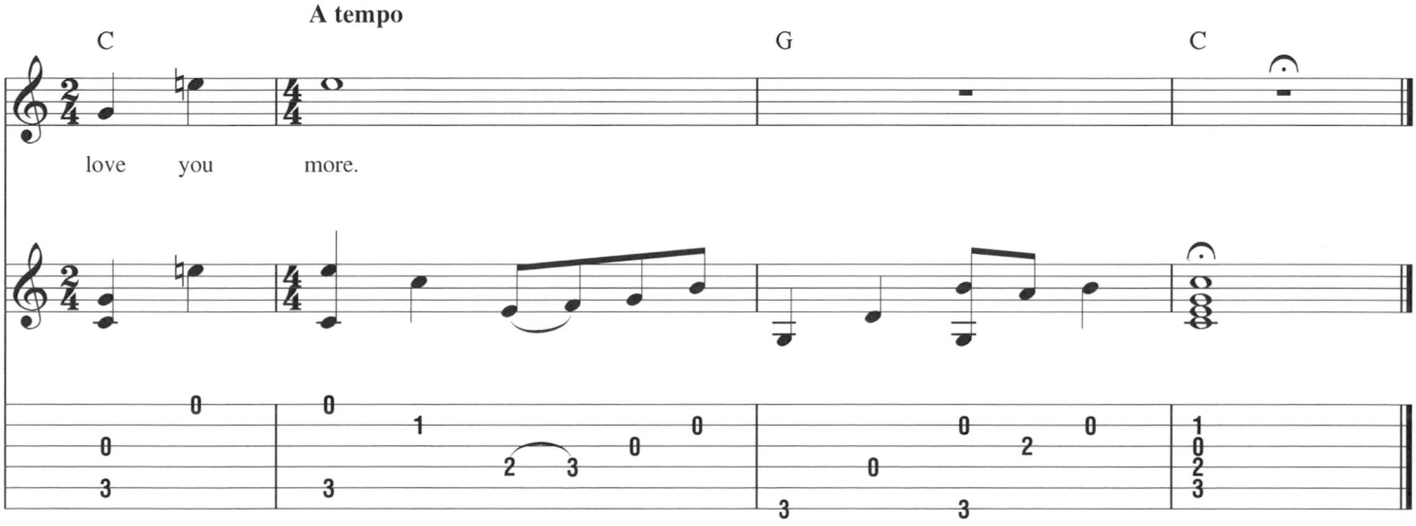
A tempo
C
G
C
love you more.

Dust in the Wind

Words and Music by Kerry Livgren

© 1977, 1978 EMI BLACKWOOD MUSIC INC. and DON KIRSHNER MUSIC
All Rights Controlled and Administered by EMI BLACKWOOD MUSIC INC.
All Rights Reserved International Copyright Secured Used by Permission

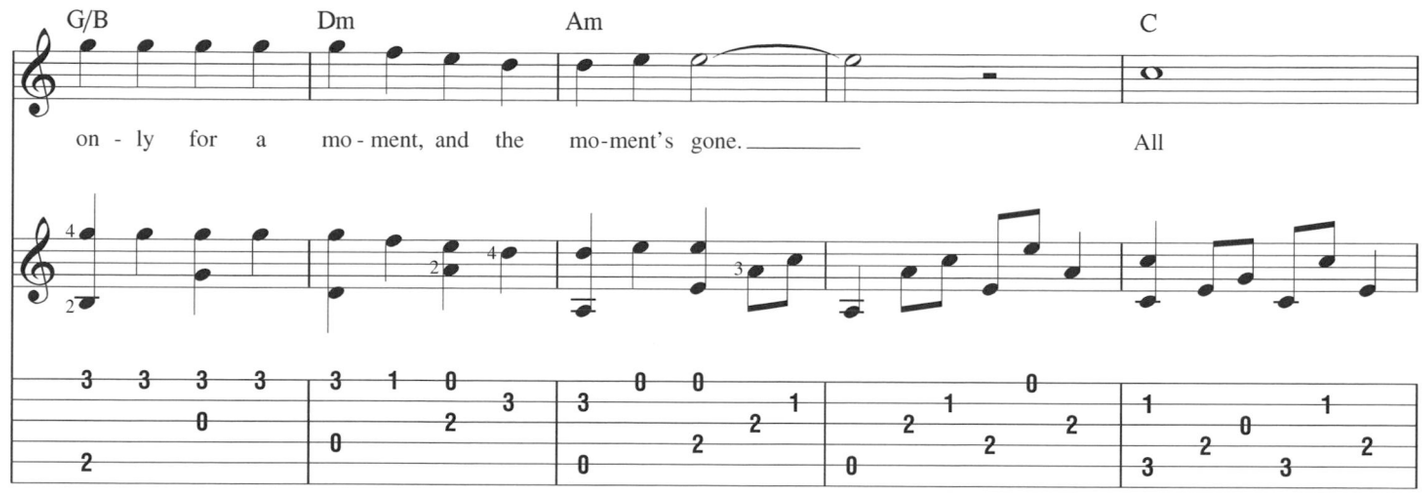
G/B
Dm
Am
C
on - ly for a mo - ment, and the mo-ment's gone.
All

G/B
Am
G/B
Dm
my dreams
pass be - fore my eyes a cu - ri -

Chorus
Am
D/F♯
G
Am
os - i - ty.
Dust in the wind.

1.
Am/G
D/F♯
G
Am
G/B
All they are is dust in the wind.

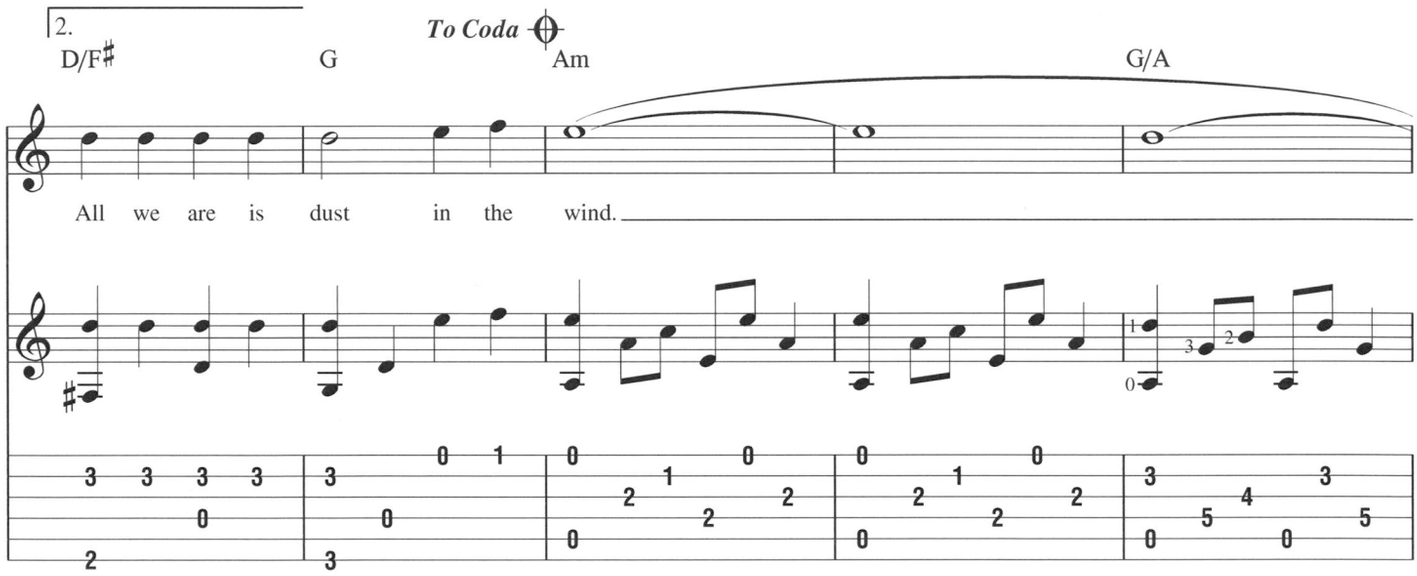
2.
To Coda
D/F♯
G
Am
G/A
All we are is dust in the wind.

D.C. al Coda
(take 2nd ending)
F/A
Oh, oh, oh.
1/3CI

Additional Lyrics

2. Same old song,
   Just a drop of water in an endless sea.
   All we do
   Crumbles to the ground though we refuse to see.

3. Now, don't hang on,
   Nothing lasts forever but the earth and sky.
   It slips away,
   And all your money won't another minute buy.

Helplessly Hoping

Words and Music by Stephen Stills

Copyright © 1969 Gold Hill Music Inc.
Copyright Renewed
All Rights Administered by Sony/ATV Music Publishing, 8 Music Square West, Nashville, TN 37203
International Copyright Secured All Rights Reserved

D
Am
- ing a word.
Gasp - ing at glimp - ses of
C
G
D
gen - tle true spir-it, he runs,
wish-ing he could fly,
Am7
C
G
on - ly to trip at the sound of good - bye.
D
Verse
Am
C
2. Word - less - ly watch - ing, he waits by the
3. Stand by the stair - way, you'll see some-thing

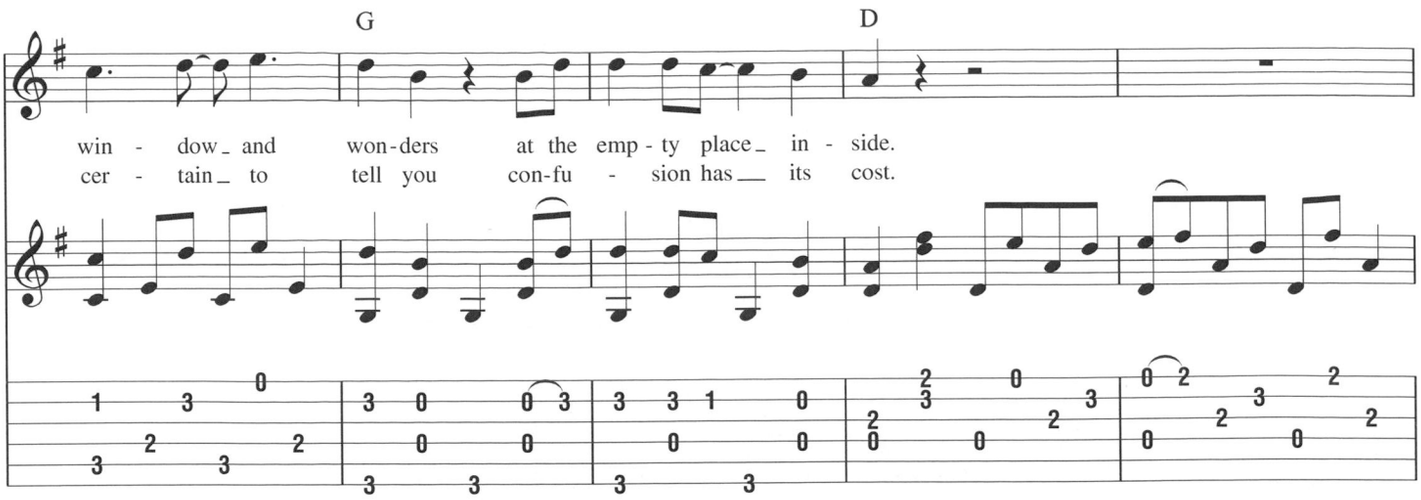
G
D
win - dow and won-ders at the emp - ty place in - side.
cer - tain to tell you con-fu - sion has its cost.

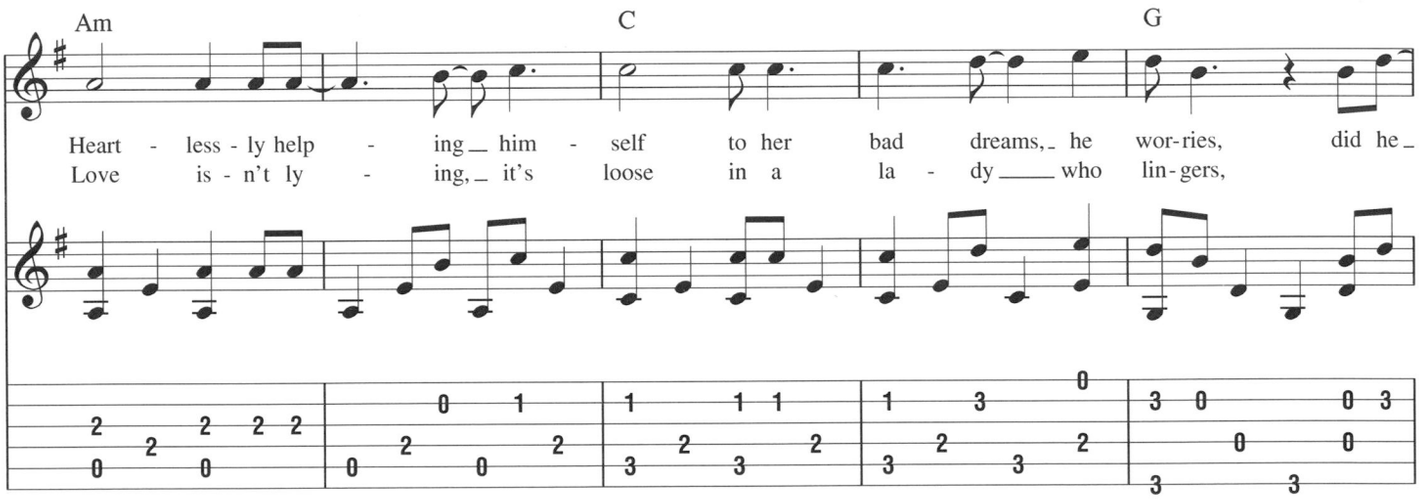
Am
C
G
Heart - less - ly help - ing him - self to her bad dreams, he wor-ries, did he
Love is - n't ly - ing, it's loose in a la - dy who lin-gers,

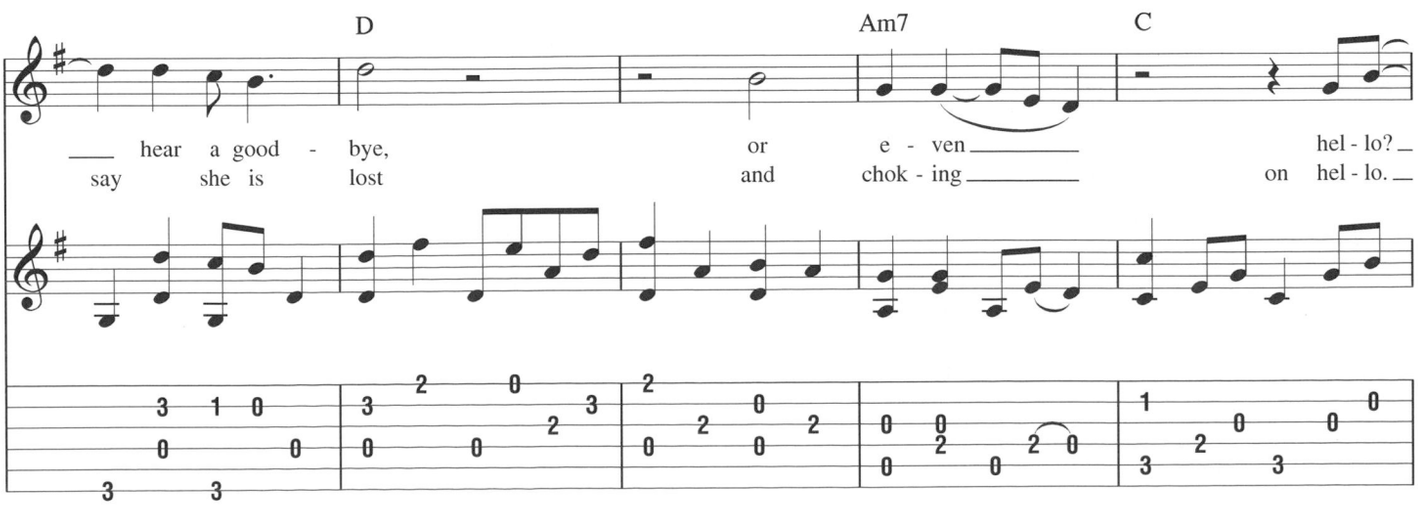
D
Am7
C
hear a good - bye, or e - ven hel - lo?
say she is lost and chok - ing on hel - lo.

Chorus
G
G7sus4
G
They are one person, they are two alone.
They are three together, they are for each
Dm/F
C
G
1.
2.
other.

Hey Jude

Words and Music by John Lennon and Paul McCartney

Copyright © 1968 Sony/ATV Songs LLC
Copyright Renewed
All Rights Administered by Sony/ATV Music Publishing, 8 Music Square West, Nashville, TN 37203
International Copyright Secured All Rights Reserved

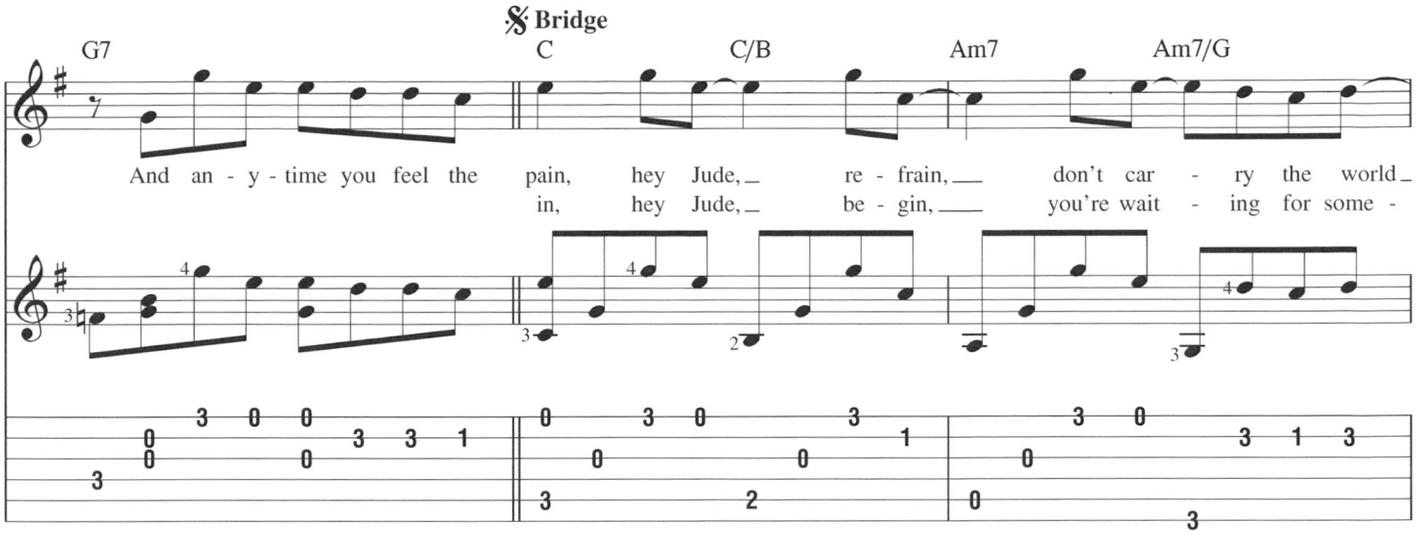
Bridge
G7
C
C/B
Am7
Am7/G
And an - y - time you feel the pain, hey Jude, re - frain, don't car - ry the world
in, hey Jude, be - gin, you're wait - ing for some -

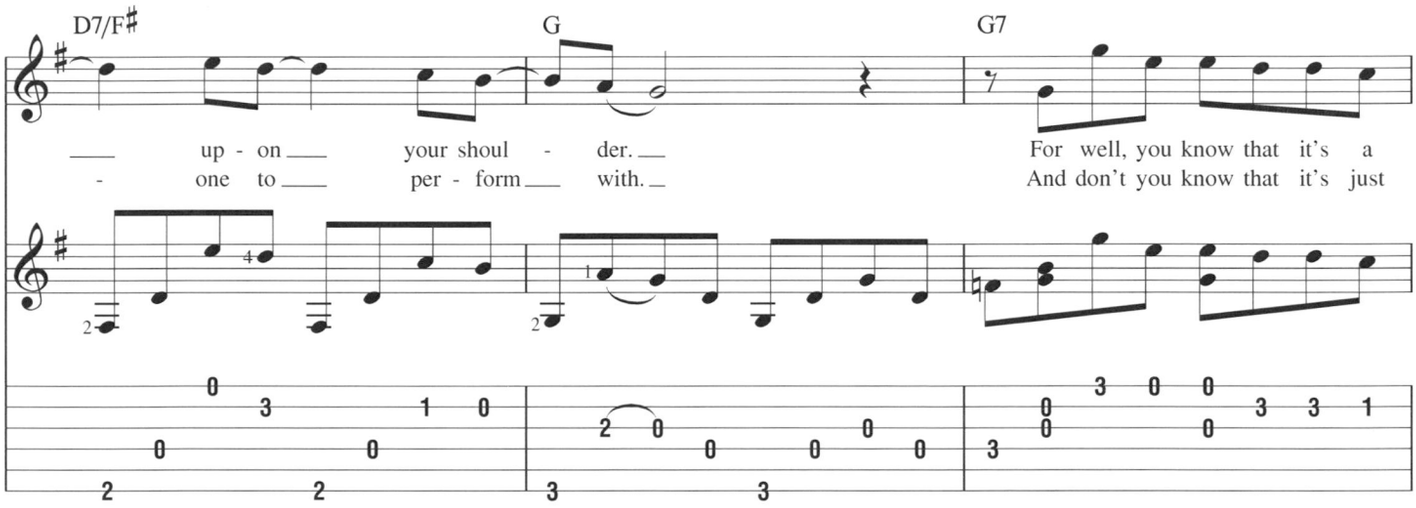
D7/F♯
G
G7
up - on your shoul - der.
- one to per - form with.
For well, you know that it's a
And don't you know that it's just

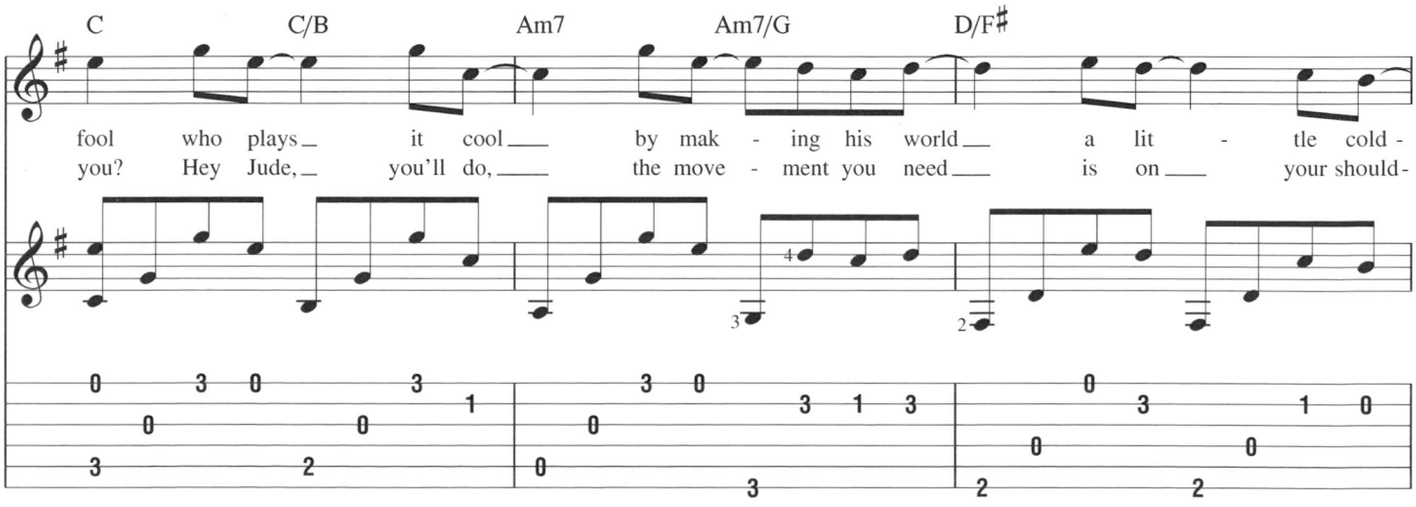
C
C/B
Am7
Am7/G
D/F♯
fool who plays it cool by mak - ing his world a lit - tle cold -
you? Hey Jude, you'll do, the move - ment you need is on your should -

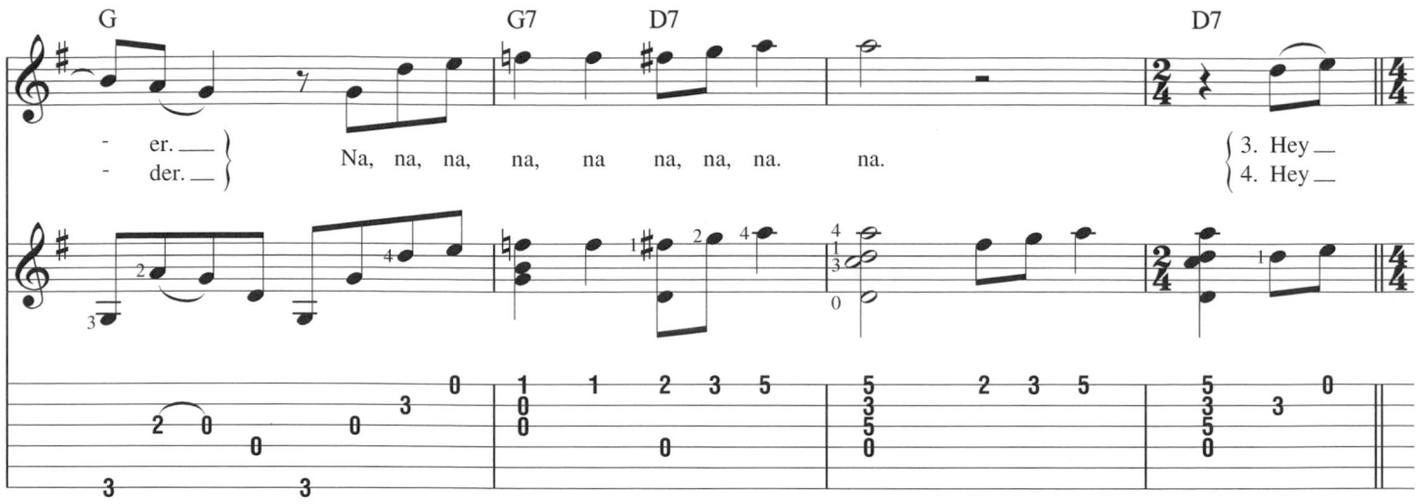
G
G7
D7
D7
- er.
- der.
Na, na, na, na, na na, na, na. na.
3. Hey
4. Hey

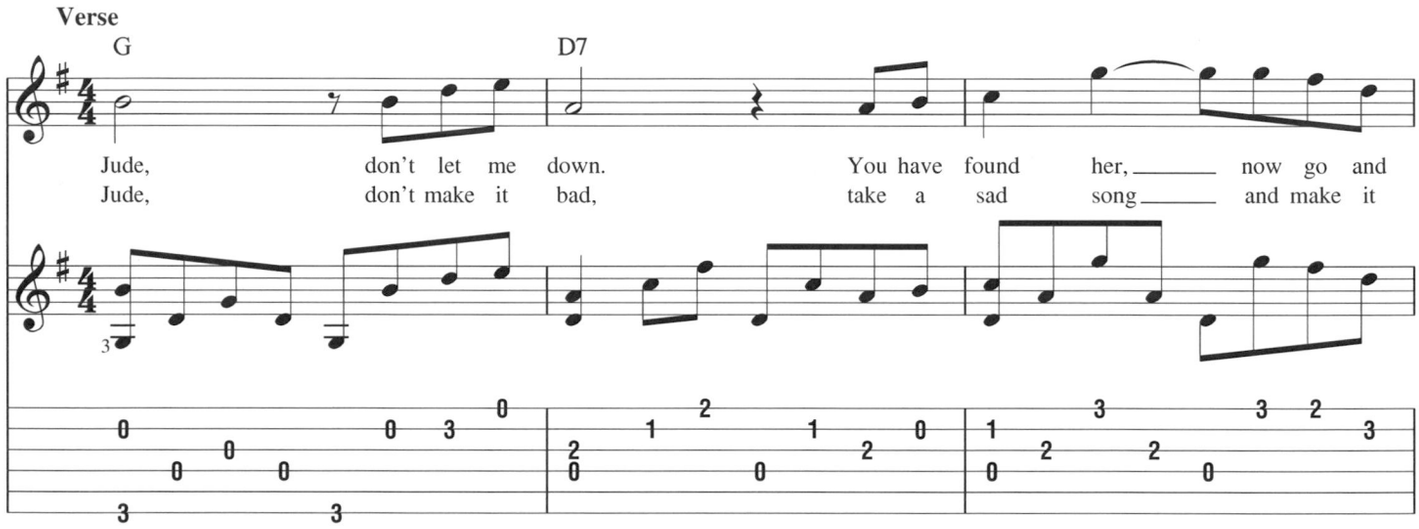
Verse
G
D7
Jude, don't let me down. You have found her, now go and
Jude, don't make it bad, take a sad song and make it

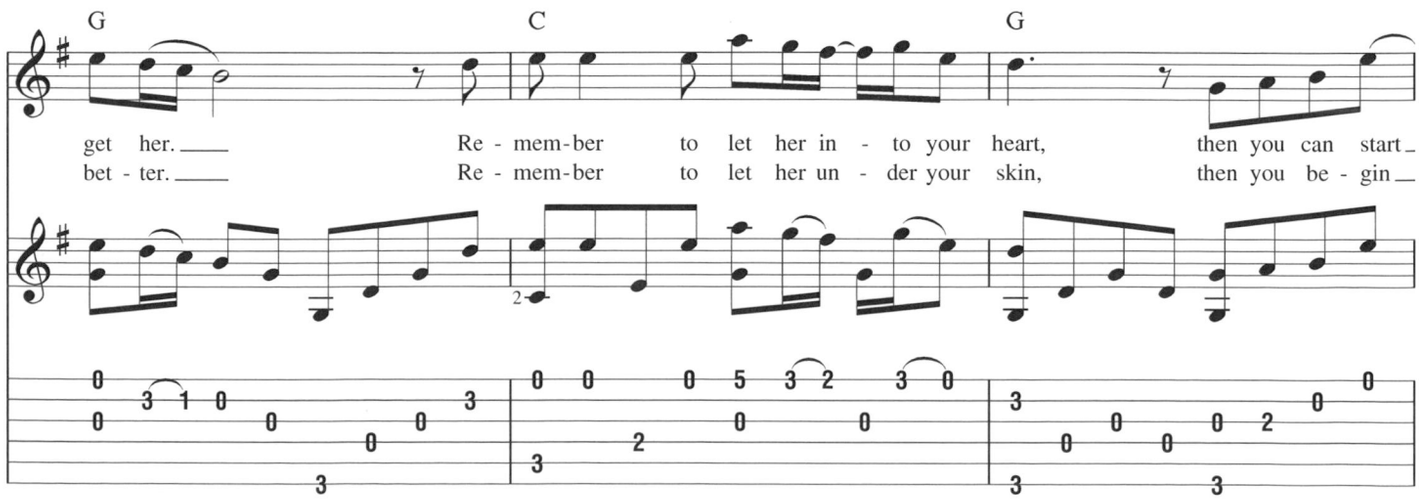
G
C
G
get her. Re - mem-ber to let her in - to your heart, then you can start
bet - ter. Re - mem-ber to let her un - der your skin, then you be - gin

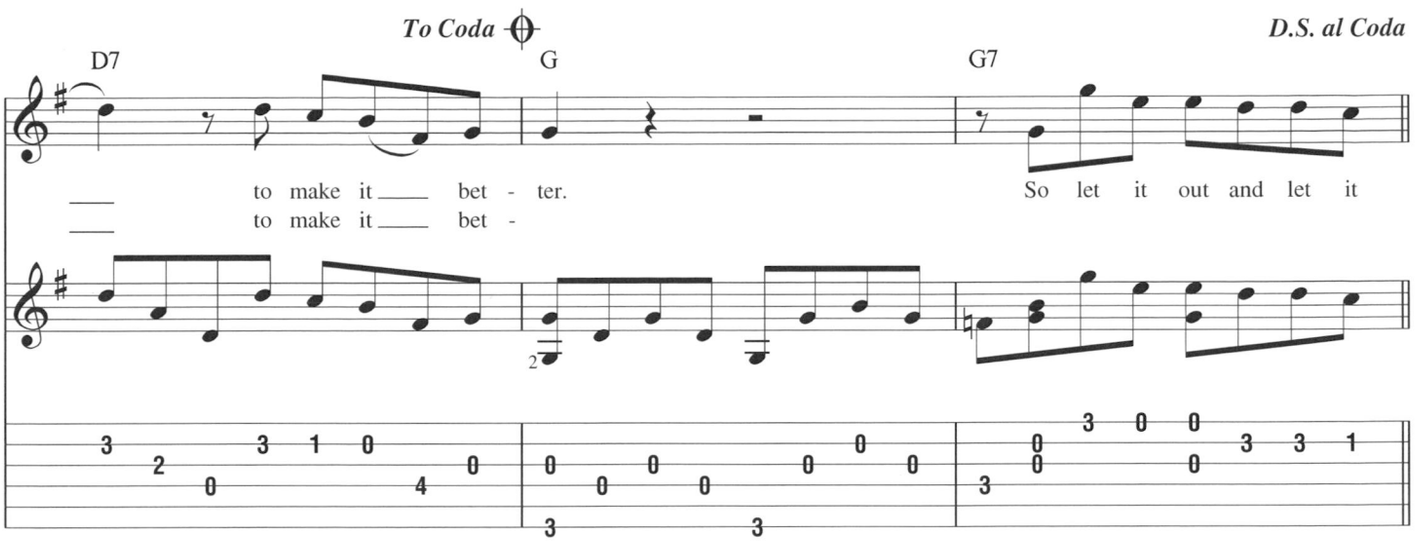
To Coda
D.S. al Coda
D7
G
G7
to make it bet - ter.
to make it bet -
So let it out and let it

Coda
Outro
G
G
ter, bet - ter, bet - ter, bet - ter, bet - ter, bet - ter, oh!
Na, na, na, na,

Repeat and fade
F
C
G
na, na, na, na,
na, na, na, na,
hey, Jude.

Learning to Fly

Words and Music by Jeff Lynne and Tom Petty

(c) 1991 EMI APRIL MUSIC INC. and GONE GATOR MUSIC
All Rights Reserved International Copyright Secured Used by Permission

F C Am G F C
start - ed out all a - lone.
break your heart, steal your crown.

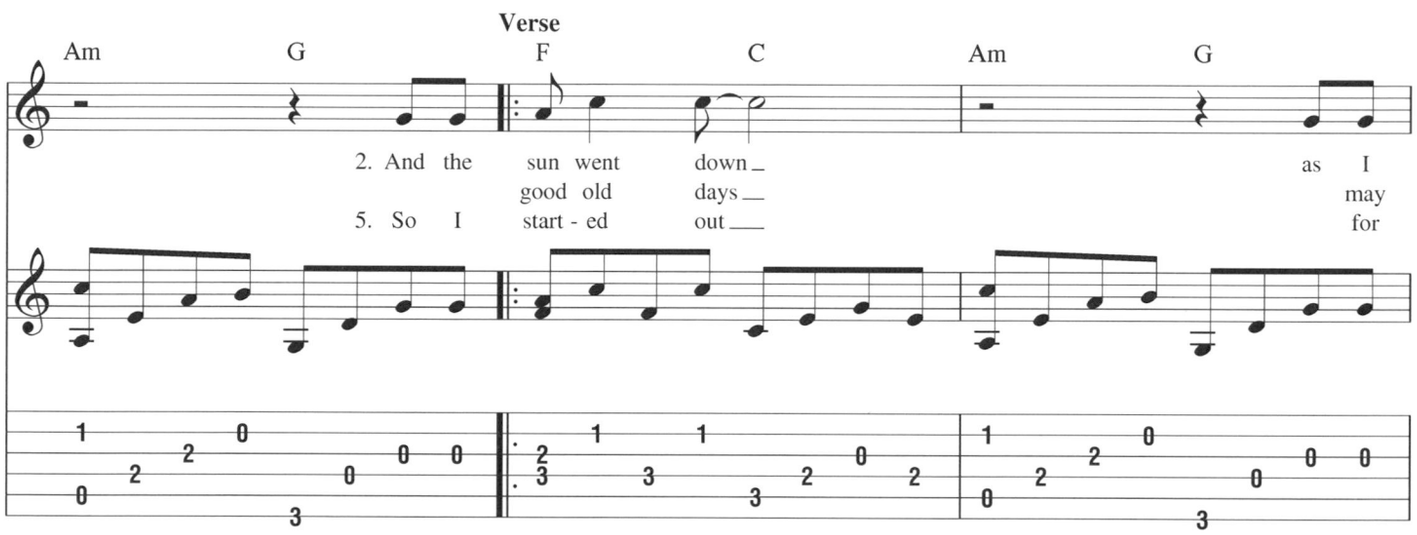
Verse
Am G F C Am G
2. And the sun went down as I
good old days may
5. So I start - ed out for

F C Am G F C
crossed the hill and the town lit up,
not re - turn, and the rocks might melt,
God knows where. I guess I'll know

Am G F C Am G
the world got still.
and the sea may burn.
when I get there.
1., 2. I'm
3. I'm

Chorus

F C Am G F C
learn - ing to fly,
learn - ing to fly,
but I ain't got wings.
a - round the clouds.

Am G F C Am G
Com - ing down
What goes up
is the

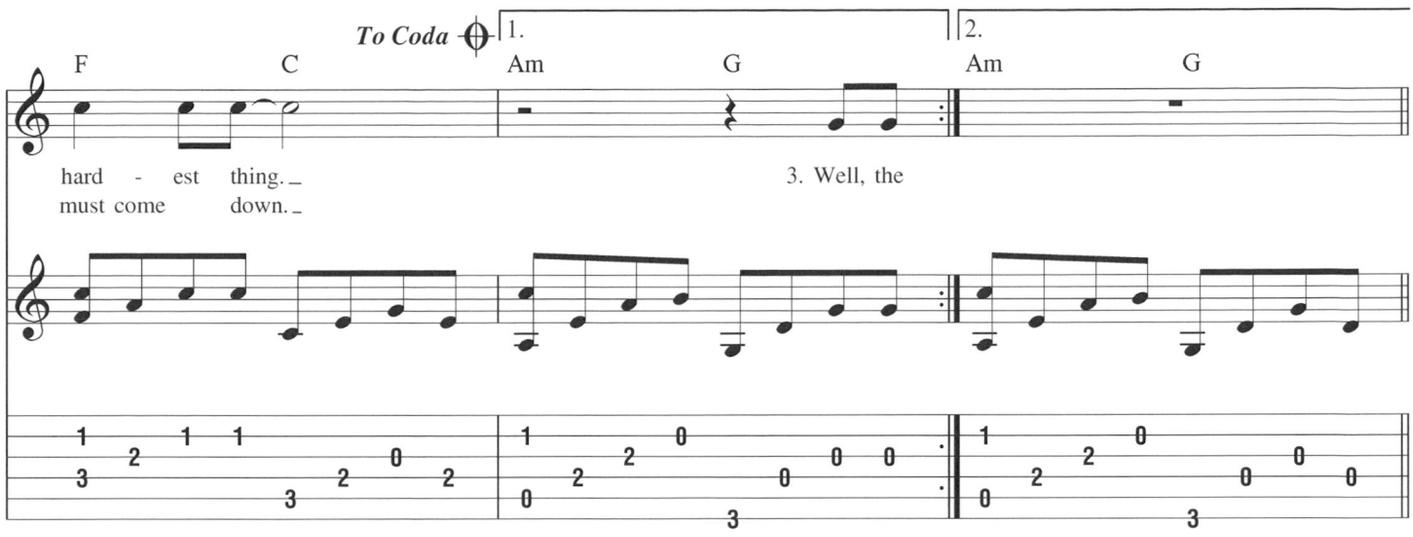
To Coda
1.
2.
F
C
Am
G
Am
G
hard - est thing.
must come down.
3. Well, the

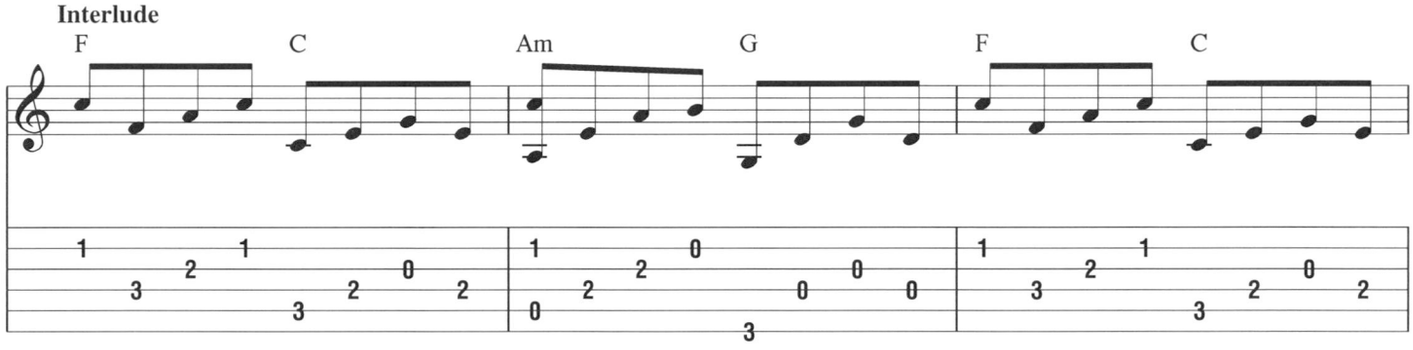
Interlude
F
C
Am
G
F
C

D.S. al Coda
Am
G
4. Well,

Coda
Outro-Chorus
Am
G
F
C
I'm
learn-ing to fly,
learn-ing to fly,
learn-ing to fly.

Am G F C Am G
but I ain't got wings.
a - round the clouds.

F C Am G F C
Com - ing down
What goes up
Learn - ing to fly.
is the hard - est thing.
must come down.

1., 2.
3.
Am G Am G C
I'm
I'm

Leaving on a Jet Plane

Words and Music by John Denver

Copyright © 1967 Cherry Lane Music Publishing Company, Inc. (ASCAP) and DreamWorks Songs (ASCAP)
Rights for DreamWorks Songs Administered by Cherry Lane Music Publishing Company, Inc.
International Copyright Secured All Rights Reserved

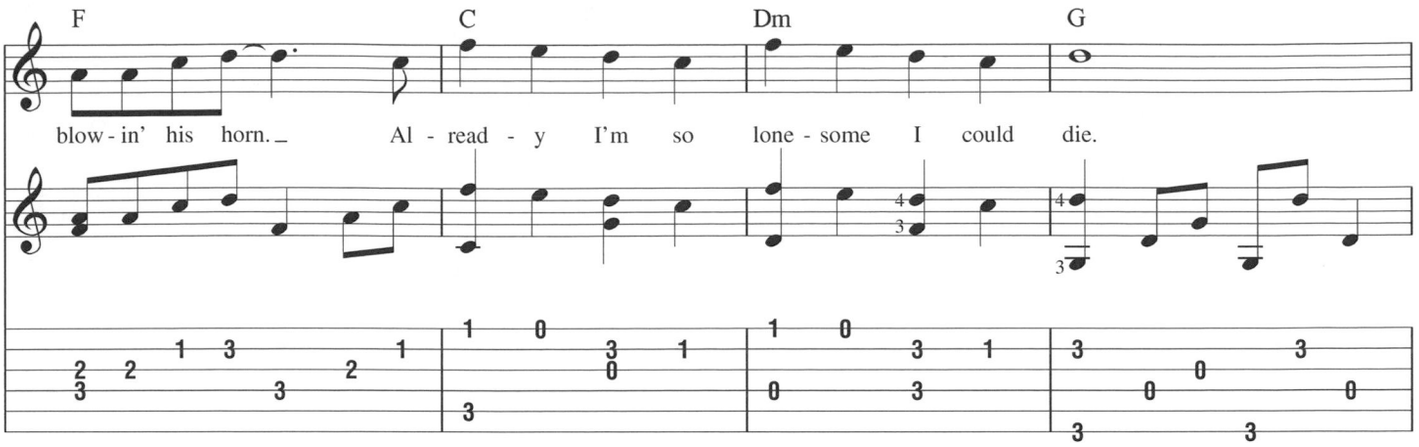
F C Dm G
blow - in' his horn. Al - read - y I'm so lone - some I could die.

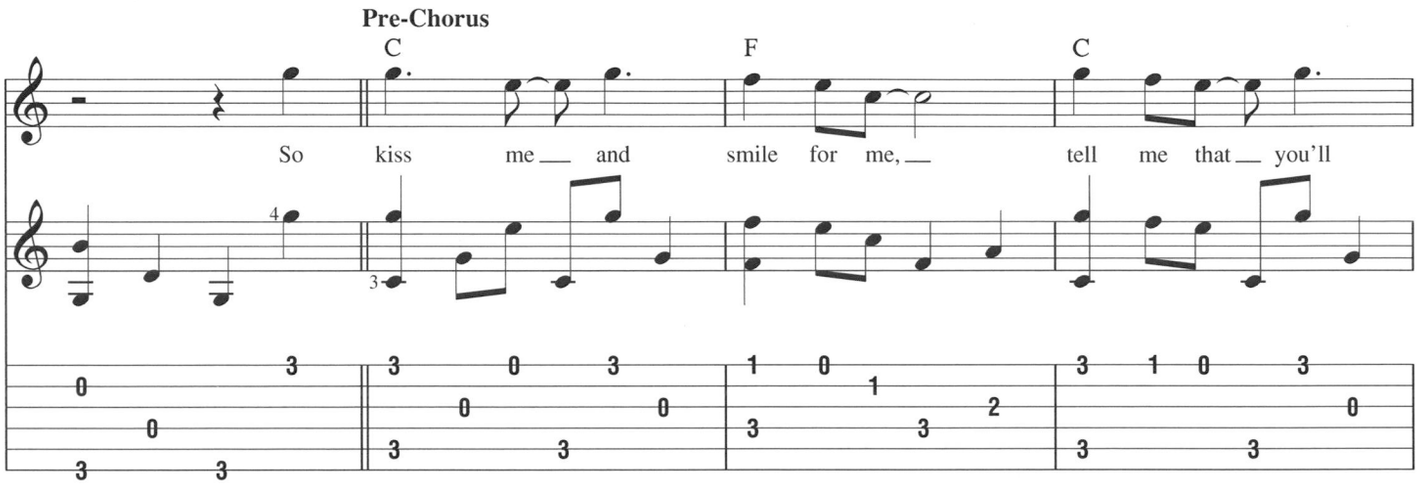
Pre-Chorus
C F C
So kiss me and smile for me, tell me that you'll

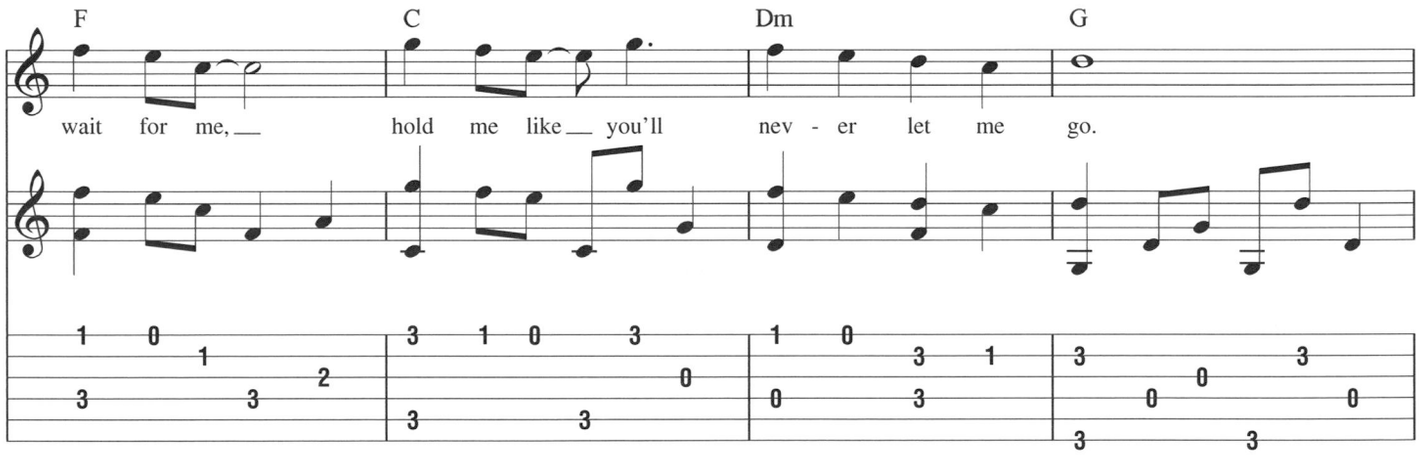
F C Dm G
wait for me, hold me like you'll nev - er let me go.

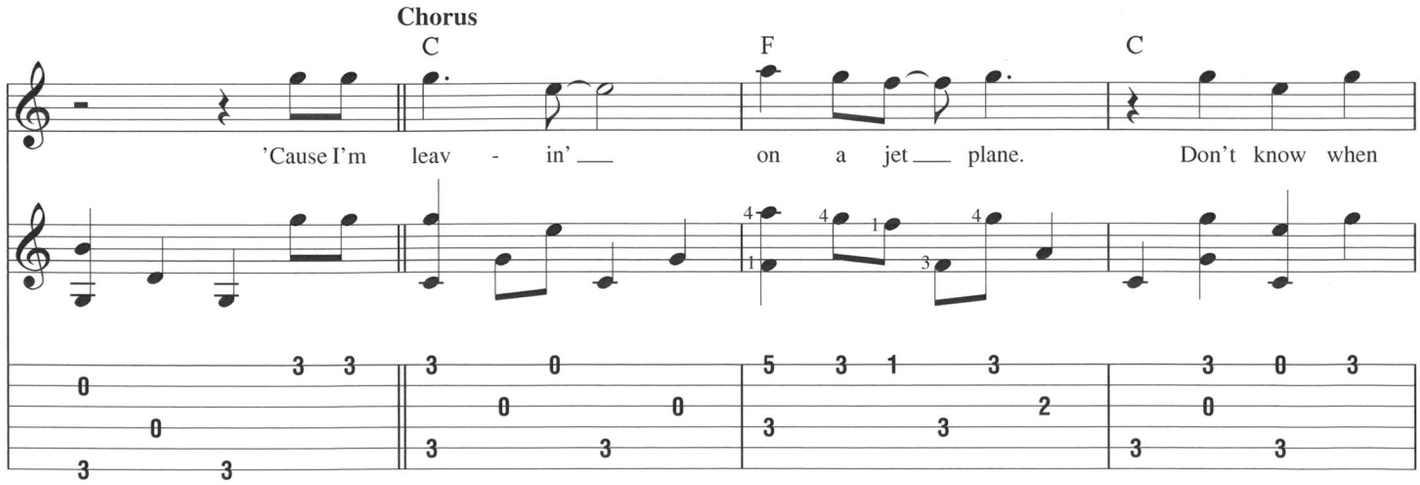
Chorus
C F C
'Cause I'm leav - in' on a jet plane. Don't know when

Additional Lyrics

2. There's so many times I've let you down,
So many times I've played around.
I tell you now, they don't mean a thing.
Ev'ry place I go, I'll think of you,
Ev'ry song I sing, I'll sing for you.
When I come back, I'll wear your wedding ring.

3. Now the time has come to leave you,
One more time let me kiss you.
Then close your eyes, I'll be on my way.
Dream about the days to come,
When I won't have to leave alone,
About the times I won't have to say...

Patience

Words and Music by W. Axl Rose, Slash, Izzy Stradlin', Duff McKagan and Steven Adler

Copyright © 1988 Guns N' Roses Music (ASCAP)
International Copyright Secured All Rights Reserved

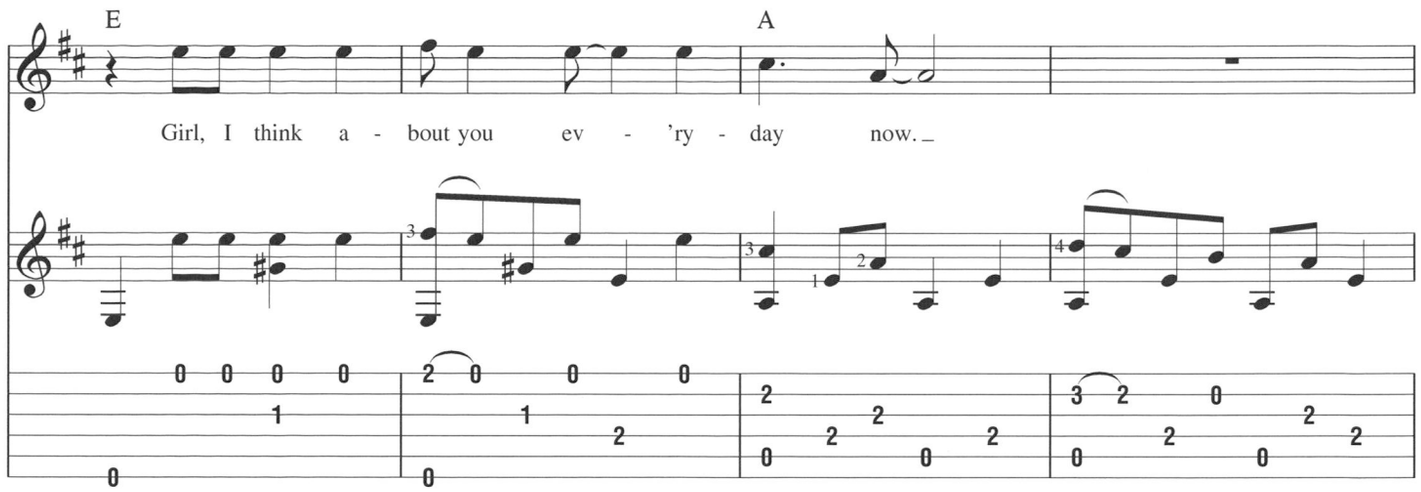
E
A
Girl, I think a - bout you ev - 'ry - day now.

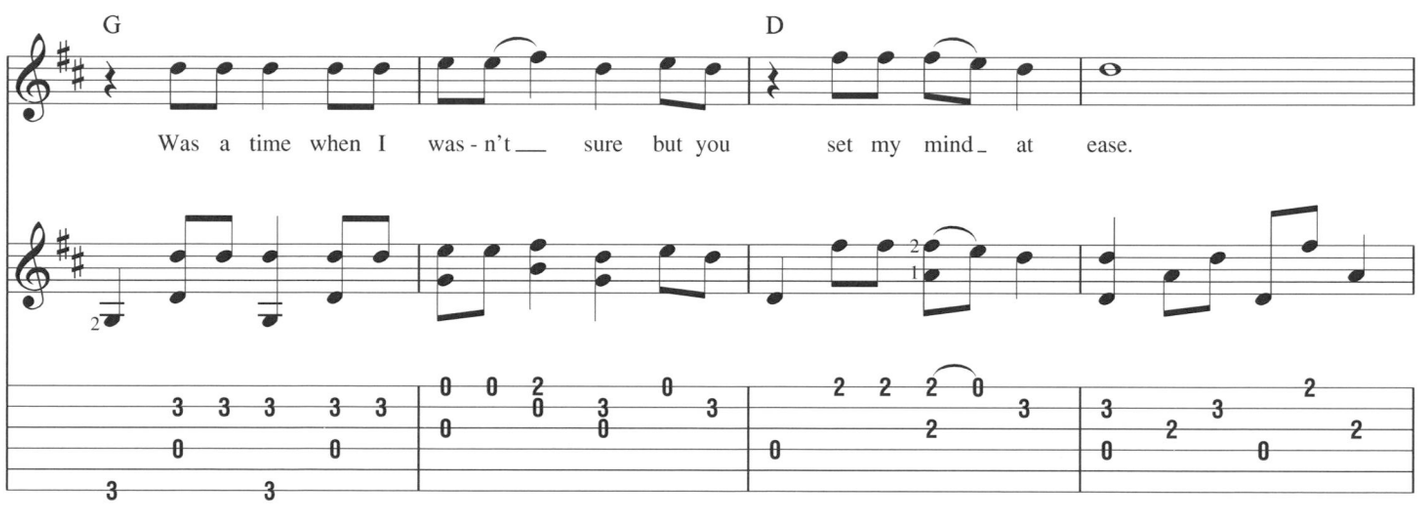
G
D
Was a time when I was - n't sure but you set my mind at ease.

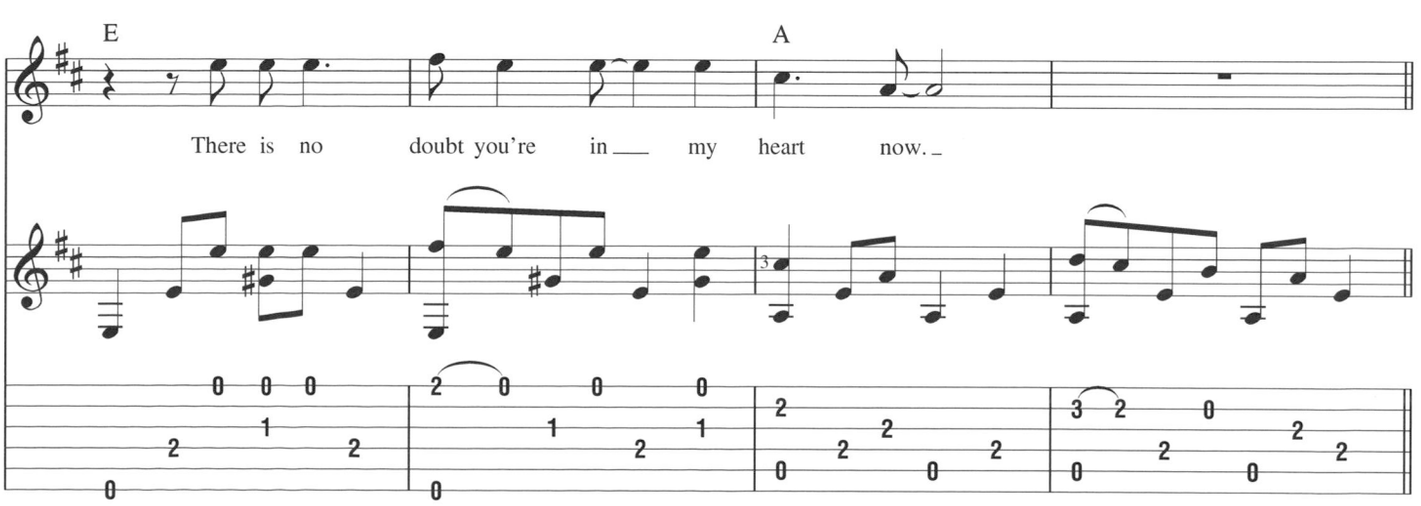
E
A
There is no doubt you're in my heart now.

Chorus
G
D
G
Said wom - an, take it slow, it - 'll work it - self out
Bm
G
D
fine. All we need is just a lit - tle
A
G
pa - tience.
Said sug - ar,

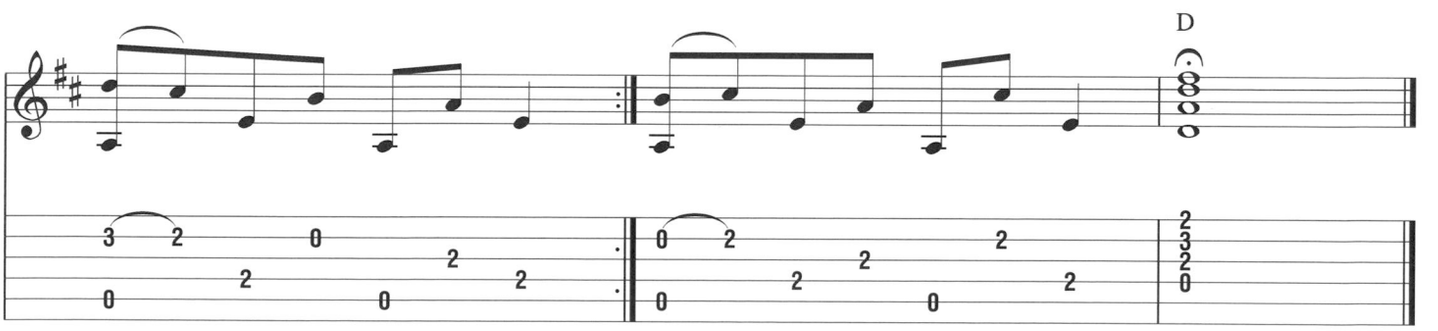

Additional Lyrics

2. I sit here on the stairs 'cause I'd rather be alone.
   If I can't have you right now I'll wait, dear.
   Sometimes I get so tense but I can't speed up the time.
   But you know, love, there's one more thing to consider.

Tears in Heaven

Words and Music by Eric Clapton and Will Jennings

Copyright © 1992 by E.C. Music Ltd. and Blue Sky Rider Songs
All Rights for E.C. Music Ltd. Administered by Unichappell Music Inc.
All Rights for Blue Sky Rider Songs Administered by Irving Music, Inc.
International Copyright Secured All Rights Reserved

Chorus
F
C
G
Am
if I saw you in heav - en?
if I saw you in heav - en?
1., 4. I must be strong
2. I'll find my way
3. Be - yond the door

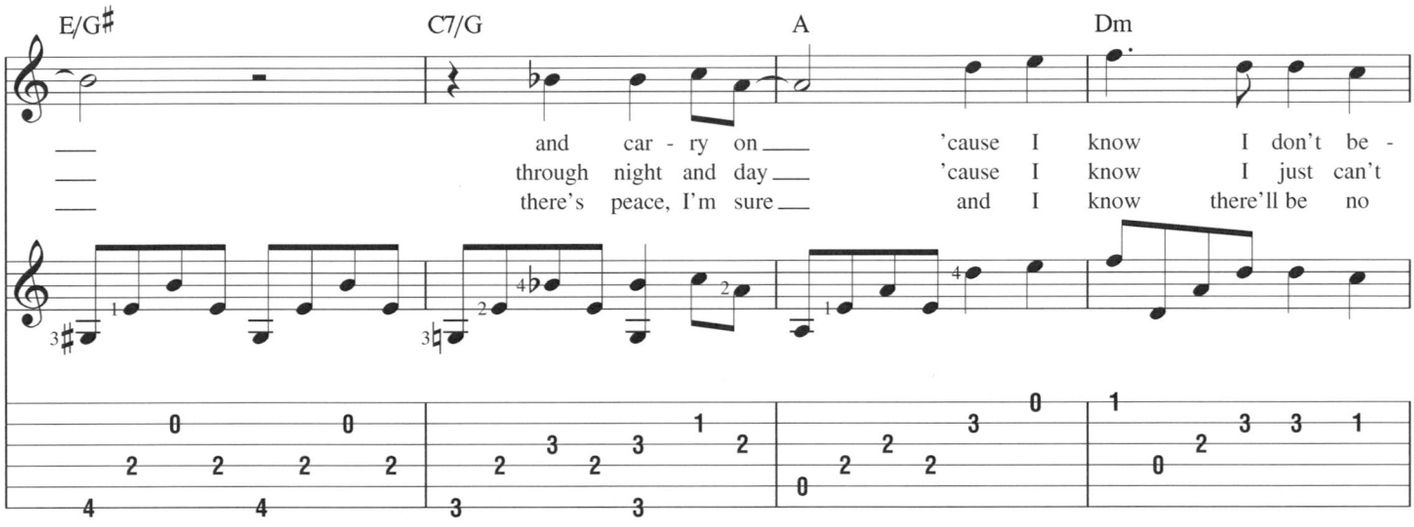
E/G♯
C7/G
A
Dm
and car - ry on
through night and day
there's peace, I'm sure
'cause I know I don't be -
'cause I know I just can't
and I know there'll be no

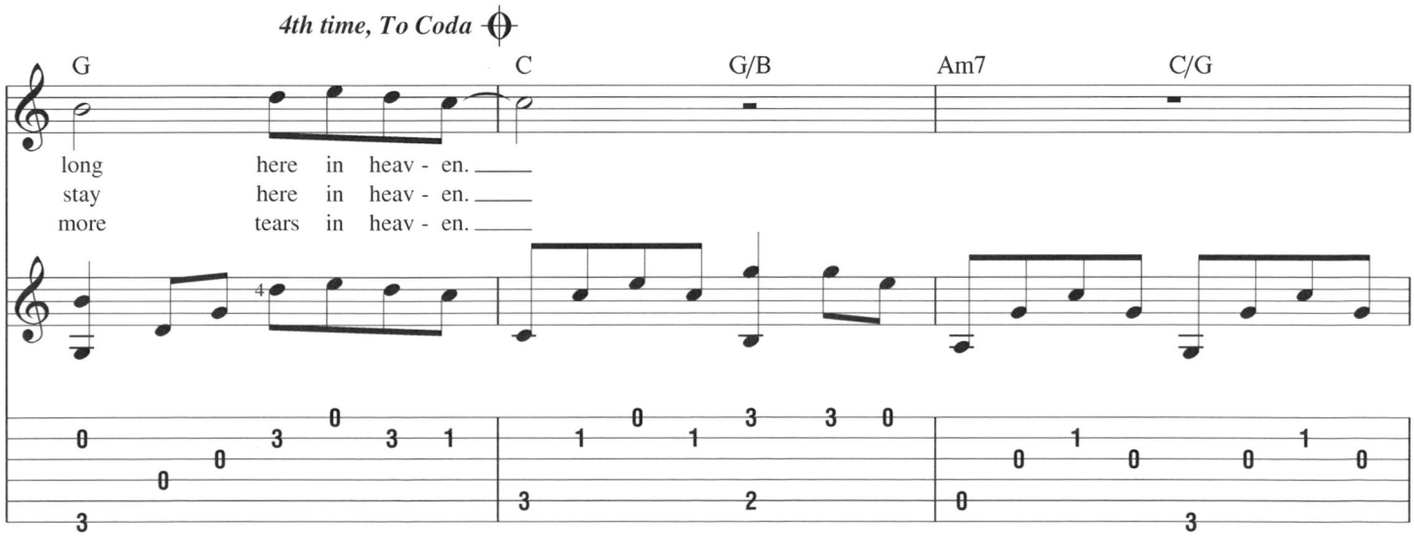
4th time, To Coda
G
C
G/B
Am7
C/G
long here in heav - en.
stay here in heav - en.
more tears in heav - en.

Bridge

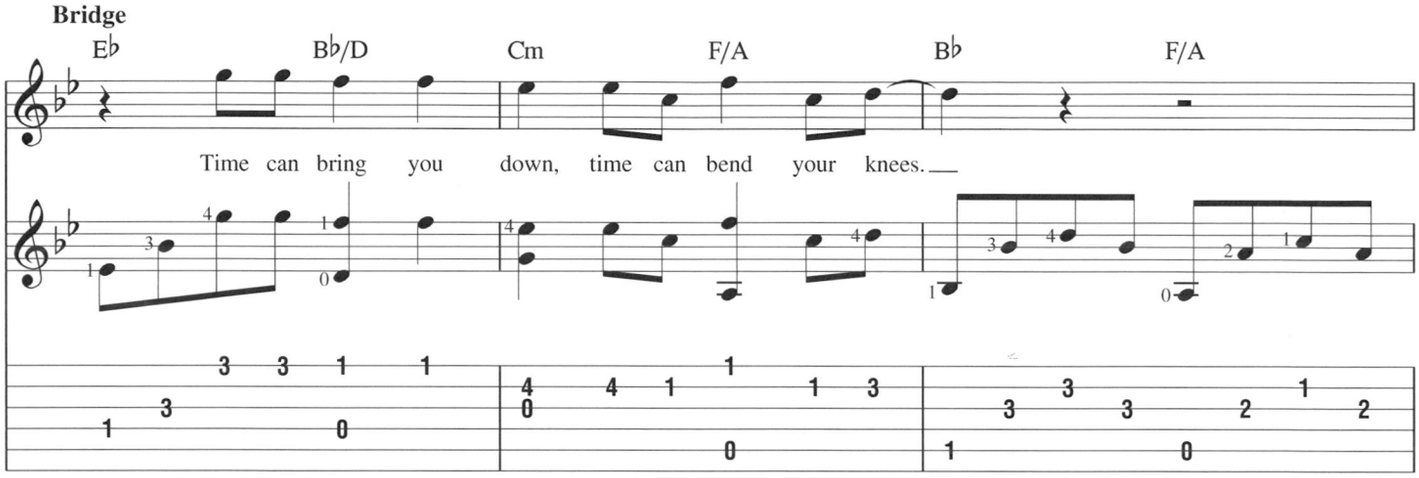

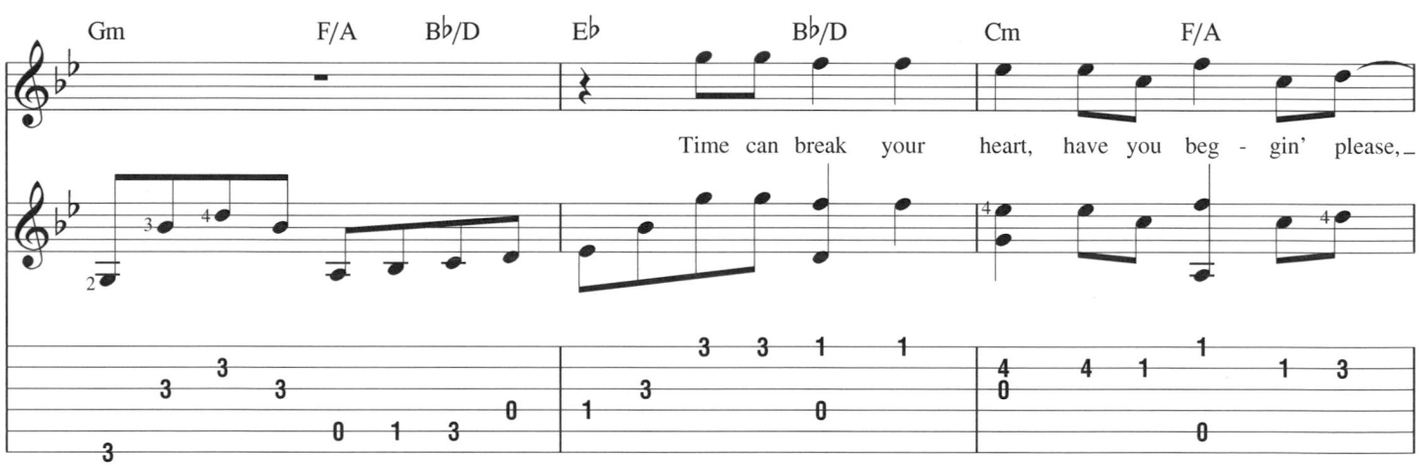

Interlude

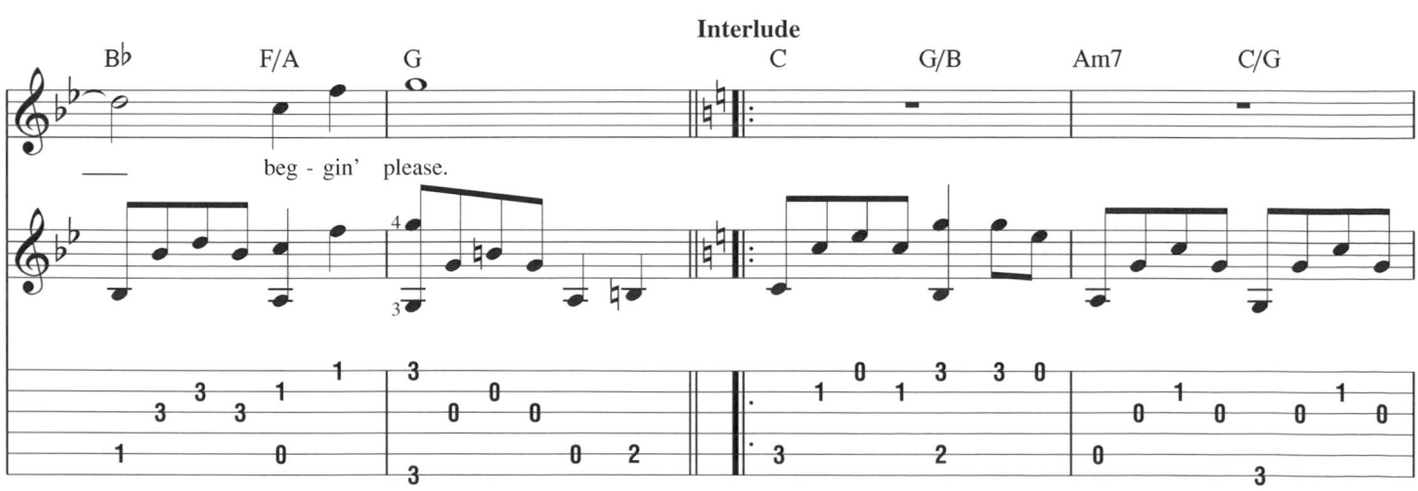

2nd time, D.S. al Coda
(take repeat)
F
C
G
Coda
C
G/B
Am7
C/G
Dm
G
'Cause I know I don't be - long here in heav - en.
C
G/B
Am7
C/G
F
rit.
Gsus4
G
C
rit.

This Land Is Your Land

Words and Music by Woody Guthrie

TRO - © Copyright 1956 (Renewed), 1958 (Renewed), 1970 (Renewed) and 1972 (Renewed) Ludlow Music, Inc., New York, NY
International Copyright Secured
All Rights Reserved Including Public Performance For Profit
Used by Permission

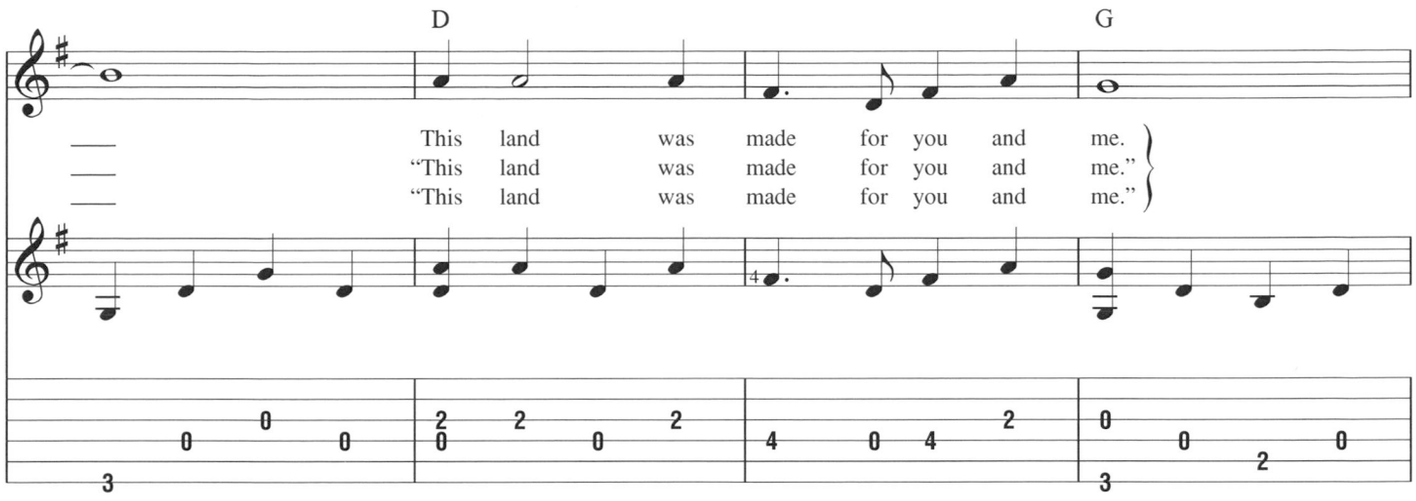
D
G
This land was made for you and me.
"This land was made for you and me."
"This land was made for you and me."

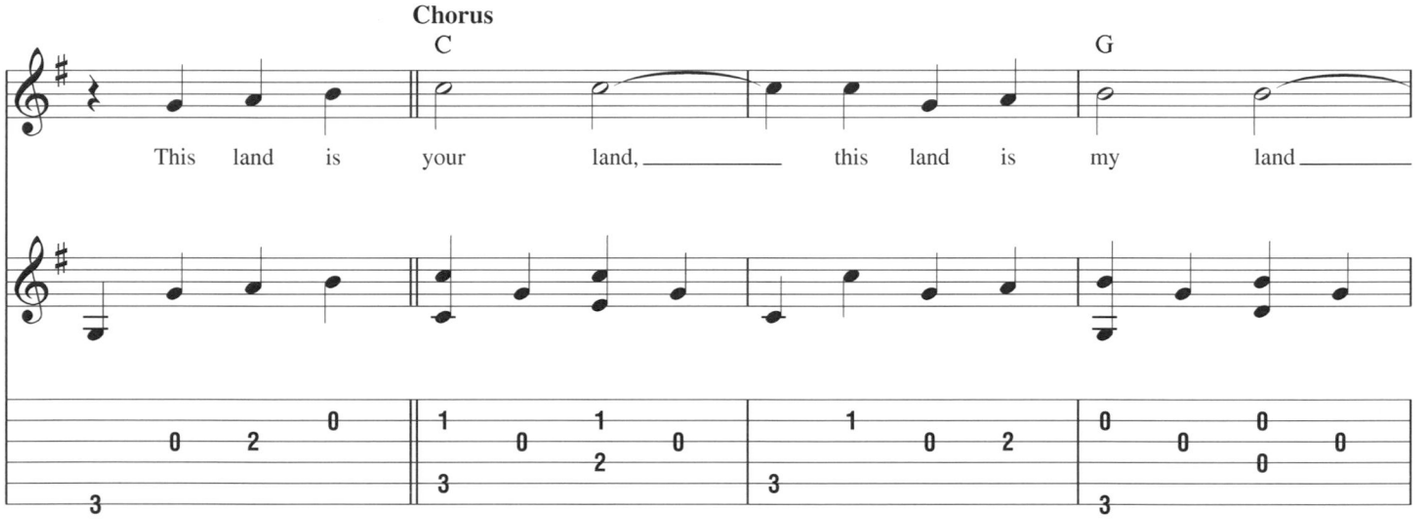
Chorus
C
G
This land is your land, this land is my land

D
G
from Cal - i - for - nia to the New York is - land.

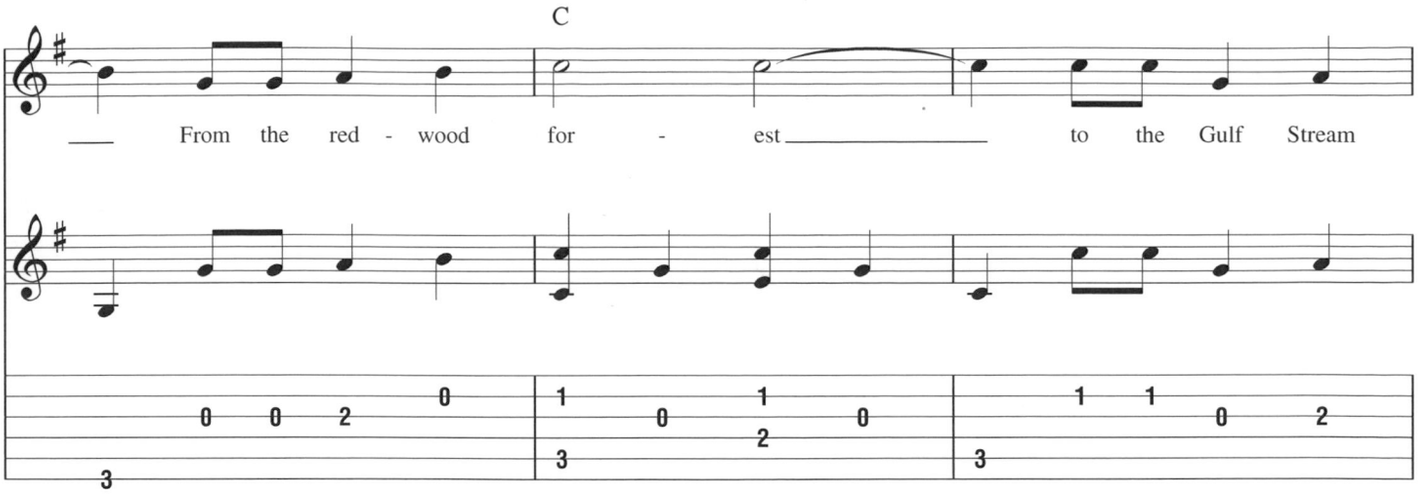
C
From the red - wood for - est to the Gulf Stream

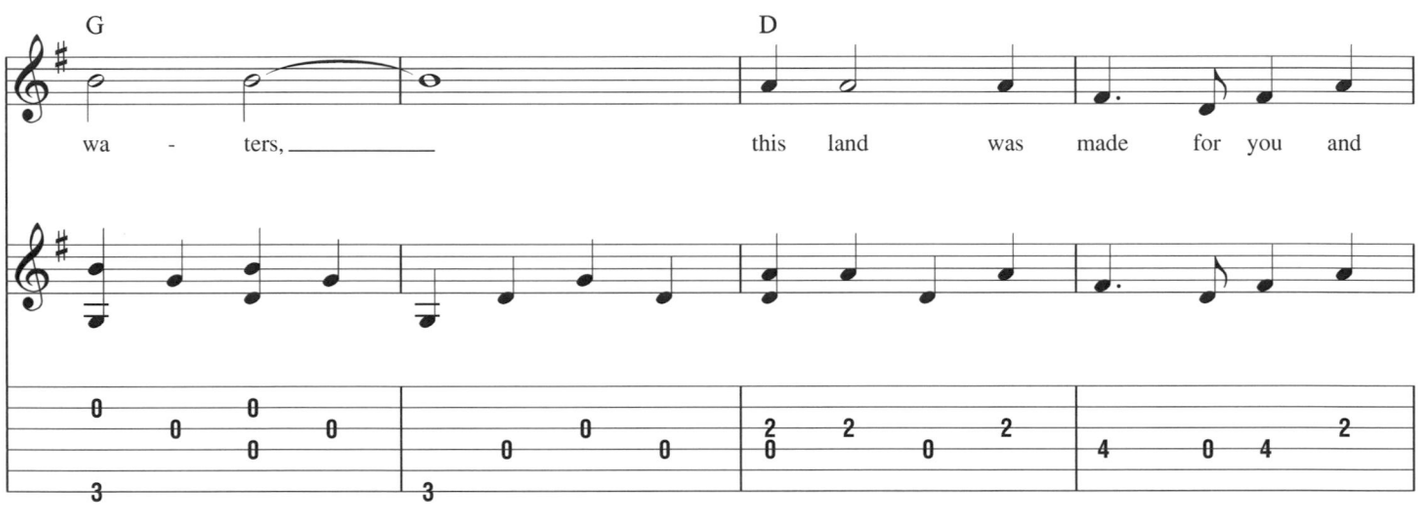
G
D
wa - ters, this land was made for you and

1., 2., 3.
4.
G
G
me.
2. I've roamed and
3. Well, the sun came
me.

Time in a Bottle

Words and Music by Jim Croce

Copyright © 1971 (Renewed) Time In A Bottle and Croce Publishing (ASCAP)
All Rights Reserved Used by Permission

E
Am
I'd like to do. is to save ev - 'ry
Am7
F
Dm
Am
day till e - ter - ni - ty pass - es a - way just to
Dm
E
1.
2.
spend them with you. 2. If But there
Chorus
A
A/G♯
F♯m7
A/E
nev - er seems to be e - nough time to do the things you want to do once you

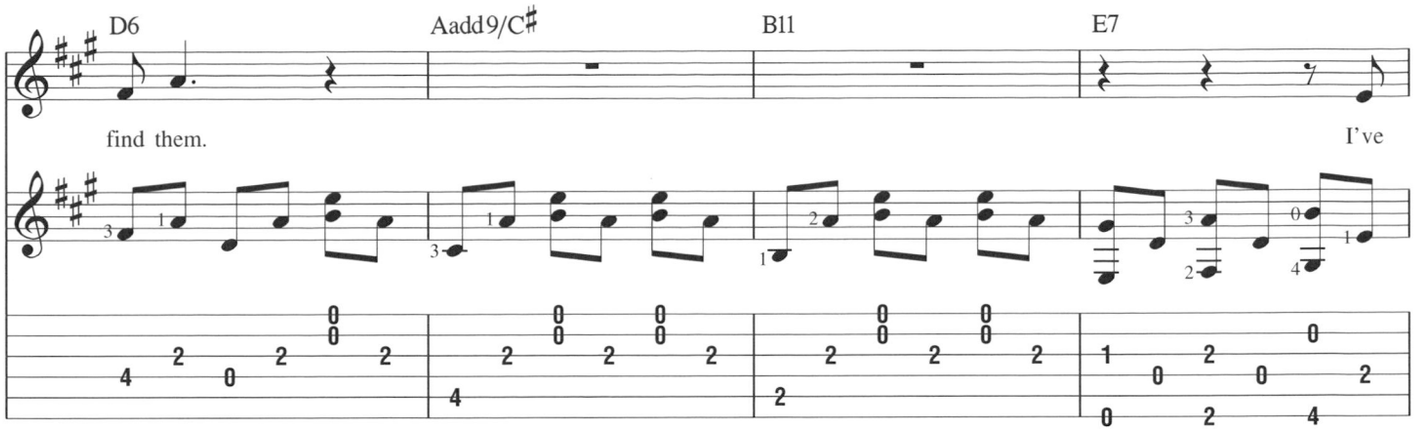

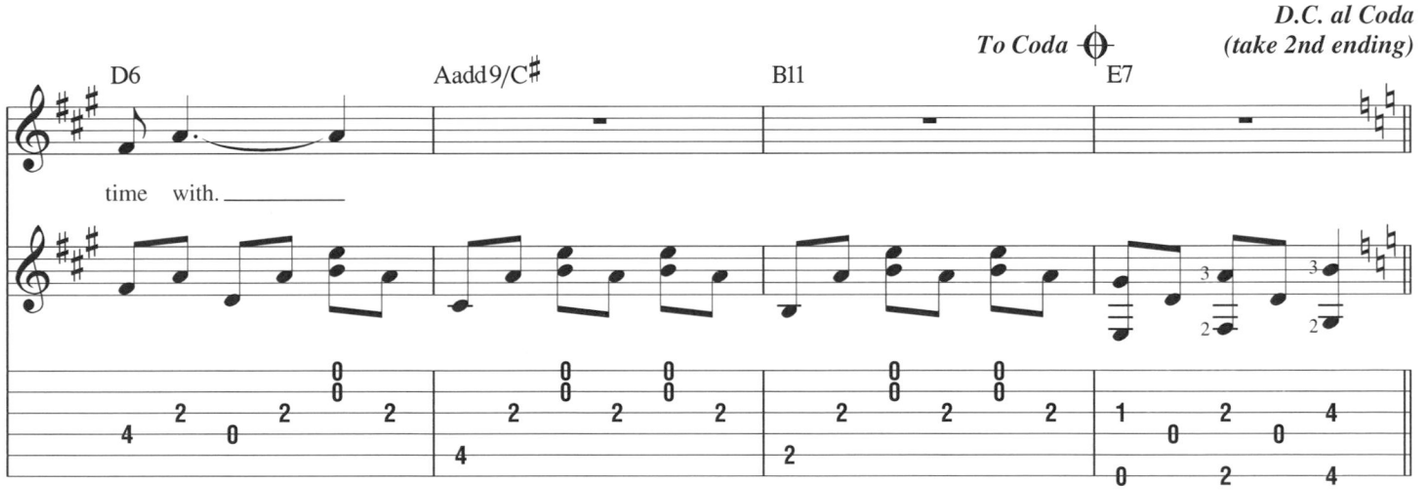

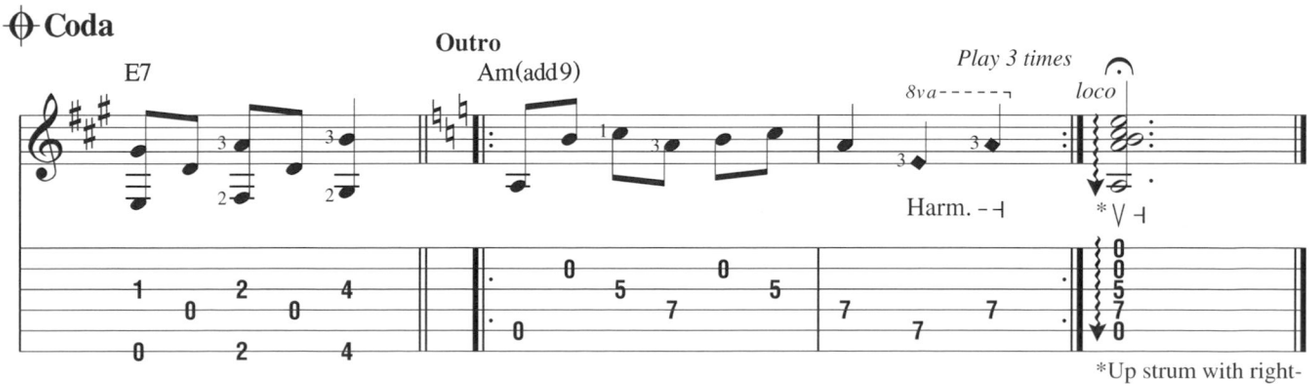

*Up strum with right-hand index finger.

Additional Lyrics

2. If I could make days last forever,
If words could make wishes come true,
I'd save ev'ry day like a treasure, and then
Again I would spend them with you.

3. If I had a box just for wishes,
And dreams that had never come ture,
The box would be empty except for the mem'ry
Of how they were answered by you.

You've Got a Friend

Words and Music by Carole King

© 1971 (Renewed 1999) COLGEMS-EMI MUSIC INC.
All Rights Reserved International Copyright Secured Used by Permission

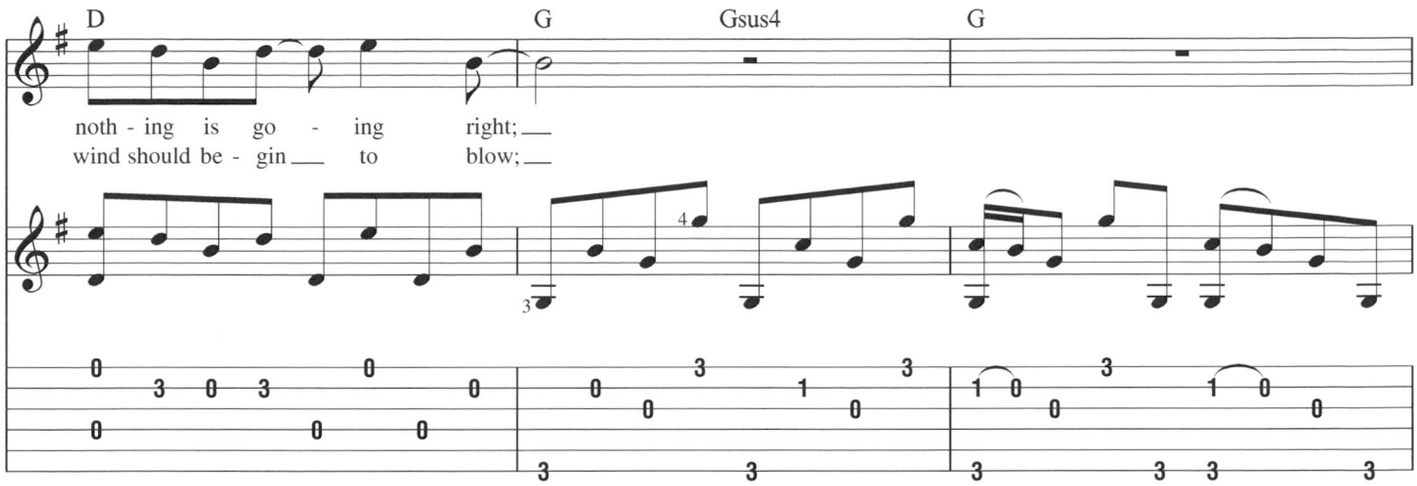
D G Gsus4 G
noth - ing is go - ing right;
wind should be - gin to blow;

F♯m7 B7 Em B7
close your eyes and think of me, and soon I will be
keep you head to - geth - er and call my name out

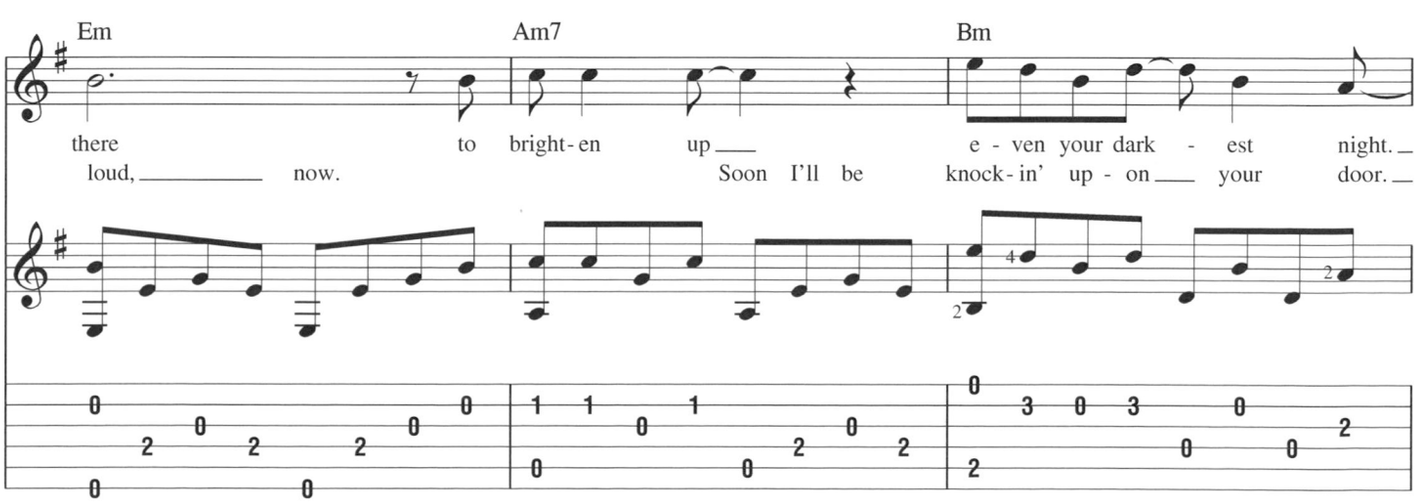
Em Am7 Bm
there to bright-en up e - ven your dark - est night.
loud, now. Soon I'll be knock-in' up - on your door.

D7sus4
Chorus
G
You just call out my name,
C
and you know wher - ev - er I am, I'll come
G
run - ning to see you a - gain.
D7sus4
G
Gmaj7
Win - ter, spring, sum - mer or fall,

To Coda
1.
C
Em7
Cmaj7
Bm
all you have to do is call, and I'll be there, yeah, yeah,
1/2CV
D7sus4
G
C
C/D
yeah. You've got a friend.
G
F♯m7
B7
Cmaj7
Bm
2.
2. If the sky be there, yeah, yeah,
1/2CV
Bridge
D7sus4
F
C
yeah. Hey, ain't it good to know that you've got a friend when

G
Gmaj7
C
peo - ple can be so cold? They'll hurt you and de - sert
F
Em
A7
you. Well, they'll take your soul if you let them. Oh, yeah but
D7sus4
D7
D.S. al Coda
don't you let them. You just call
Coda
Cmaj7
Bm
Dsus4
G
be there, yes, I will. You've got a friend.
1/2CV